Battle for Berlin

BATTLE

FOR

BERLIN

— Dr. Joseph Goebbels —

ANTELOPE HILL PUBLISHING

English Translation Copyright © 2024 Antelope Hill Publishing

First edition, second printing 2024.

Translated from the German *Kampf um Berlin*, published by Franz Eher Nachf, 1938.

Cover art by Swifty.
Translated by Germain Muller.
Edited by Tom Simpson.
Proofread by CJ Miller.
Layout by Sebastian Durant.

Antelope Hill Publishing | antelopehillpublishing.com

Paperback ISBN-13: 979-8-89252-032-4
Hardcover ISBN-13: 979-8-89252-033-1
EPUB ISBN-13: 979-8-89252-034-8

*I dedicate this book to the
Party's Old Guard of Berlin.*

– Dr. Joseph Goebbels –

Contents

Foreword by Thomas Dalton, PhD

Perhaps the most erudite and insightful writer of National Socialist Germany was Dr. Joseph Goebbels. His reflections on the National Socialist rise to power are second in importance only to those of Adolf Hitler himself; thus, it is worth taking a moment to reflect on his life and his role in National Socialist Germany.

Goebbels was born into a devout Catholic family on October 29th, 1897, in the town of Rheydt, near Düsseldorf. He went on to study at four universities, eventually settling at Heidelberg, where he earned a PhD in history and philology in 1921. He was a prolific scholar and writer, ultimately producing over a dozen books and several dozen articles. Goebbels apparently first took notice of Hitler and his National Socialist platform in late 1923 and began working for the National Socialist German Workers' Party by late 1924. Within a year he was editing National Socialist periodicals while working with Gregor Strasser and others of the northern branch of the Party.

Goebbels soon earned the attention of Hitler and was named *Gauleiter* (district leader) of Berlin in October 1926. It was at this very time that National Socialism engaged in the infamous "Battle for Berlin," during which the originally South German movement struggled to establish dominance in the northern capital city. This was a crucial event in the history of the young movement and is rightly the subject of the present book.

In 1927, Goebbels founded a major National Socialist periodical, *Der Angriff*, and by 1930 was promoted to Minister of Propaganda

(*Reichspropagandaleiter*). He was thus well-placed by the time Hitler and the NSDAP acceded to power in 1933. As the most intelligent and well-educated of the National Socialist leaders, he quickly rose to the highest Party levels. One observer with firsthand knowledge of the man was Hugh Wilson, US ambassador to Germany in 1938. Wilson called Goebbels "a man of high intelligence" and "an interesting and stimulating conversationalist," adding that, "among the leading men of the Nazi Party, there is none who . . . is so well able to expound the Nazi doctrine, or so competent to meet the foreigner on his own ground."

Goebbels would eventually become, along with Hitler and Hermann Göring, a member of the early leadership trinity of the Party; he would retain this power and influence through the war years and right to the very end of the Third Reich. In time he would eclipse both Göring and Heinrich Himmler, the latter of whom served more as an enforcer than actual leader. Into the 1940s, Goebbels "was the most important and influential man after Hitler. . . . [B]y 1943, he was virtually running the country while Hitler was running the war."

Hostile critics often like to condemn Goebbels for his position as Minister of Propaganda, arguing that, due to this, he cannot be trusted. But in fact, precisely the opposite is the case. Propaganda cannot be effective unless it is, by and large, true. This was acknowledged decades ago by prominent French scholar Jacques Ellul in his monumental work *Propaganda* (1962), specifically with respect to Goebbels. Early in his book, Ellul refers to "Goebbels' insistence that facts to be disseminated must be accurate." Ellul adds that Goebbels "wore the title of Big Liar . . . and yet he never stopped battling for propaganda to be as accurate as possible. He preferred being cynical and brutal to being caught in a lie." Ellul continues:

> He was always the first to announce disastrous events or difficult situations, without hiding anything. The result was a general belief, between 1939 and 1942, that German communiqués not only were more concise, clearer, and less cluttered, but were more truthful than Allied communiqués—and furthermore, that the Germans published all the news two or three days before the Allies. All this is so true that pinning the title of Big Liar on Goebbels must [itself] be considered quite a propaganda success.

This amounts to a striking endorsement of Goebbels' passion for the truth.

This is particularly so for the subject at hand: the Battle for Berlin. During 1926 and 1927, the National Socialists had many opponents to contend with: Marxists, communists, and Jews, among others. The ruling Weimar government was highly Jewish and served to promote Jewish values and Jewish interests throughout Germany, primarily via free-market capitalism. On the other hand, Jewish Marxists and communists sought to promote Bolshevism within Germany and Europe more generally, playing on their relatively recent victory in the Soviet Union. The "Red" Jewish groups were able to convince many ordinary Germans that they were fighting for the common man, and that the anticipated "revolution of the proletariat" would bring them wealth and luxury. Thus, the mass of Germans was divided between Jewish-led capitalism and Jewish-led Marxism and Bolshevism. This division presented a huge challenge for Hitler's National Socialism. This was the backdrop for the *Battle for Berlin*.

Ultimately, Hitler and Goebbels were able to make the case that German *nationalism* was more in the interests of average Germans than internationalism and that *socialism* (an economy in the service of the people) was better than capitalism (an economy in the service of rich financiers). The advantages were clear and transparent, and thus it was not hard to show that something like National Socialism was superior to globalist capitalism.

The third and final piece of the puzzle was the Jewish angle. Hitler and Goebbels could rightly show that Jews were at the forefront of both globalism and capitalism, and that they profited the most from these systems rather than regular Germans. This, again, was obvious to all; every German knew of local wealthy Jews flaunting their money, even as ordinary Germans struggled for their daily bread. Hitler solved this final problem by driving out the Jews and re-establishing a Germany for the Germans. And the results were spectacular: in six short years, Germany rose from a depressed and indebted nation to the heights of world power, both militarily and culturally.

And indeed, we face a similar situation today. In America, we have a system of internationalist, free-market capitalism, and Jews have flourished here as never before in history. The middle class is being crushed, and ever more regular Americans are driven into poverty. In Europe, the situation is somewhat more restrained, given their inclination for quasi-socialist economies, but they, too, have their wealthy Jews, and via NATO and various economic coercions, the US system holds much power over Europe.

Still, it is undoubtedly as true today as it was 100 years ago: *Nationalism* and *socialism*, combined with an exclusion of the Jews, would pave the way to spectacular successes in the Western nations. We can scarcely imagine the vast improvements in quality of life and standard of living that would ensue, should we embark on such a path. Of course, the Jews know this too, and hence, via the media and academia, they do everything in their power to demonize and disparage the very idea.

Even a very cursory review of the facts shows that Hitler was right; Goebbels was right; National Socialism was, and is, the path to a very bright future—for all but the Jews. In this light, we can truly appreciate the National Socialist "Battle for Berlin," and we can understand the urgency in Goebbels' words. He knew what was at stake, and he sensed what was to be gained. Fortunately, neither his words nor his lessons learned were lost to history. *Battle for Berlin* is an invaluable guide to all those who hope for a better future.

Thomas Dalton, PhD
2024

Translator's Preface

As the translator entrusted with bringing this historical work into a new language, I am honored to present *Battle for Berlin* by Dr. Joseph Goebbels. I set out on this journey with a profound passion for history and an unwavering commitment to preserving and sharing the narrative captured within these pages.

Battle for Berlin is a historical document that outlines the origins and development of the National Socialist movement in the German capital. It also serves as a personal account of Goebbels' role as the leader of the Berlin branch of the NSDAP, and foreshadows his role as the chief propagandist of the Third Reich, a position he would assume less than a year after writing this book.

The book was first published in 1932, when the NSDAP was still struggling to gain power in Germany. It covers the first year of Goebbels' history with the movement in Berlin as its *Gauleiter*, from 1926 to his thirtieth birthday in 1927. The book consists of Goebbels' brief introduction and then twelve chapters, each focusing on a specific event or aspect of the movement's campaign in Berlin. Some of the topics include his transfer to the Berlin NSDAP, the clashes with the communists and Social Democrats, the founding of *Der Angriff*, accounts about the Sturmabteilung, and the challenges and achievements of the movement in Berlin.

The text is written in a vivid and dramatic style, full of rhetorical devices, emotional appeals, and Goebbels' knack for sarcasm. The edition used in this translation is from 1938. The text itself is the same as the 1932 original, merely republished six years later. The author portrays himself and his comrades as heroic, determined champions fighting for a noble cause, facing overwhelming odds and formidable enemies. He depicts his foes as brutal yet cowardly antagonists who resort to violence and intimidation to suppress the National Socialist message. He also criticizes the Weimar Republic–then the regime of Germany at the time–as a thoroughly corrupt and weak system that has betrayed Germany and its people. He praises National Socialism for its unique ability to restore Germany's glory and honor where many other ideologies have failed.

The book is an interesting source of historical information, as it allows the modern reader to see the National Socialist movement through its own eyes. It is also a work of idealism and propaganda that can at times embellish facts and details. Nonetheless, it presents a historiography from an otherwise neglected point of view, that of the losing side of the Second World War. This is valuable, as history is a complex and nuanced subject matter that requires a holistic perspective if one wants to accurately and fully understand a people and its national conscience.

With this in mind, I have endeavored to bridge the gaps between the German language and culture of its time and the contemporary English-speaking world, allowing readers to explore Dr. Goebbels' profound insights into the beginnings of the National Socialist movement in Berlin. This translation is not merely a linguistic endeavor but a labor of love dedicated to making the rich tapestry of the past accessible to a wider audience.

My interest in Dr. Goebbels' work and the historical period in which it was written nurtured my desire to undertake this translation. Throughout this process, I grappled with the intricate task of balancing fidelity to the original text and intent with the need to ensure a smooth and engaging reading experience in English. It is my hope that the translation captures the nuances and spirit of the original text, inviting readers to delve more deeply into the history of National Socialism.

Concerning specific linguistic and cultural nuances I had to address during the translation, I attempted to functionally carry the intricacies into English so that the result would be meaningful to the reader, sense for sense. In other words, I wanted to produce the same relationship between the English translation and the English-speaking audience as there was with the original German text and its audience. I translated idiomatic expressions into similar English idioms;

I preserved formal and informal registers as used by the author; I tried to anglicize conventions for titles and directional addresses (unless there was a more commonly used name in English). With regard to untranslatable concepts and specific cultural and historical references, I have supplemented the translation with copious annotations of my own, so as to provide the reader with the necessary historical and contextual background to create a more robust picture of Dr. Goebbels' thoughts.

I extend my deepest gratitude to all those who have supported and inspired me throughout this endeavor. I would especially like to express my appreciation to Dr. Thomas Dalton for his helpful guidance and support throughout my translation of this historical work. His insights, expertise, and passion for the subject matter have greatly enriched the process. I am also thankful for his generous offer to contribute a foreword, adding a layer of depth and context that enhances the reader's experience. My sincere appreciation also goes out to Antelope Hill Publishing for their commitment to fostering a deeper understanding of the past. Their sponsorship of this project has made it possible for this historical narrative to reach a broader audience. I would also like to thank a few anonymous friends who helped me with interpreting more challenging phrases and rendering them in idiomatic English. Lastly, my eternal gratitude goes to my partner for all the necessary encouragement provided along the way.

Germain Muller
2024

Introduction

The battle for a capital city is always a special period in the history of revolutionary movements. The capital is an abstract concept in itself. It represents the center of all political, intellectual, economic, and cultural forces in the country. From there, its emanations exude into the provinces, leaving no town, no village untouched.

Berlin is unique in Germany: the population of this city is not composed, like that of any other, of a unified, self-contained, homogeneous mass. The Berliner is a result of old "Berlin-ness" blended with influences from new arrivals from all provinces, regions, classes, professions, and religions.

Berlin is admittedly not, as Paris is for France, the decisive pioneer in everything for all of Germany. Nonetheless, one still cannot imagine the country without Berlin.

The National Socialist movement did not originate in Berlin. It is originally from Munich. From there, it first gripped Bavaria and southern Germany and only after it left behind the beginnings of its nascent stage did it build a bridge to northern Germany and thereby to Berlin.

The history of the NSDAP north of the Main begins only after its collapse in 1923.[1] However, from then on, National Socialism

---

[1] In November 1923, after an unsuccessful coup attempt in Munich dubbed the Beer Hall Putsch, the NSDAP was legally banned until Adolf Hitler convinced the Bavarian authorities to lift its prohibition in February 1925. While banned, it operated in a fractured manner under the name Nationalsozialistische Freiheitspartei (English: "National Socialist Freedom Party").

1

continued on in northern Germany with the full vehemence of Prussian tenacity and discipline.

The object of this book is to present the history of the movement in the Reich's capital. However, it does not pursue any historical purpose whatsoever. It will be left to later historians to record the objective chronology of the movement's development in Berlin. We lack the sober detachment necessary to separate light from shadow fairly.

The author of this book himself has played a leading role in and was decisively influential on the way the course of events unfolded. He is therefore an interested party in every sense of the word. He cherishes the hope that with this book he might relieve his soul of the burden of responsibility that has encumbered him over the course of half a decade of struggle. It should be support and encouragement for those who fought in and secured the brilliant rise of the Berlin movement; for those doubting and unsympathetic onlookers, an exhortation and pang of conscience; and for those who stood against our victorious march, a threat and declaration of war.

We are not yet able to celebrate the end of this momentous struggle as a total victory.[2] May this book help to keep the hope and faith of the marching battalions of the National Socialist awakening strong, so that the goal, today already understood with clarity and consistency, never goes out of sight and is ultimately fulfilled despite everything!

Dr. Joseph Goebbels
Munich, 1932

---

[2] *Battle for Berlin* was first published in 1932, one year before the National Socialists assumed power in Germany, although this version was translated from the fourteenth edition, published in 1938.

1. Arrival in the Capital

A November morning dawns upon the large, deserted hall of the Elberfeld train station. It is now time to take leave of a city that for two years had been the starting point of the difficult and deadly battle for the Ruhr.[3] Here, in northwestern Germany, we had established the first regional headquarters of the rising National Socialist movement after 1923. The spiritual center of National Socialism in western Germany was based in Elberfeld, and from here the rays of our passionate struggle penetrated into the Ruhr.

A few comrades had come to say goodbye. In fact, this farewell was more painful than we had expected. To be torn away from an environment that has become near and dear to one through many memories of struggle and success is quite something. It all began here. Here, the first rally campaigns for the Rhineland and Ruhr were organized. Here, we had established the first citadel for the National Socialist bastions that were forming sporadically throughout the province.

The station manager has just now given the signal for departure. A quick wave, a firm handshake. My good Benno, a wonderful German shepherd who was with us in good times and bad, bays one last

---

[3] The Ruhr is a region of coal mining and heavy industry in western Germany. The Ruhr River flows through the region, from which it takes its name. The Ruhr was occupied by French troops for over two years from 1923 to 1925 after Germany defaulted on war reparation payments. The foreign occupation contributed to the momentum of the National Socialist movement in Germany.

mournful farewell, and then the train pulls out of the station concourse with a long jerk.

We race through the country at speed, swallowed up by a gray rainy twilight. Through the sites of industry and bustling activity, past the towering billowing chimneys. How often, back then, we took this route, back when we ventured into the Ruhr in the evenings to batter the communists in their own strongholds. How many times we attacked here, suffered a gruesome defeat, came back to be sent home again with more bruises and wounds, only to fight them a third time and secure a firm footing in a dogged breakthrough.

Essen! Bochum! Düsseldorf! Hagen! Hattingen! We first fortified our positions in these areas. In those days, no rally could be held without violently overcoming the Marxist terrorists. If the enemy had realized how weak we were, he presumably would have beaten us to a pulp. It was only due to the extraordinary audacity of a few Sturmabteilung soldiers that we were able to force our way into these regions at all.[4]

Our intention was to absolutely conquer a city here and there given favorable conditions. Then we would transform it into a stronghold for the rising movement, from which we could take the fight into the surrounding countryside.

One such stronghold was the small industrial town of Hattingen, situated between Bochum and Essen; a number of favorable conditions resulted in exceptionally fertile soil for us there, which we then tilled with painstaking diligence and courageous tenacity and sowed with the seeds of our young ideology. Hattingen is a medium-sized town in the Ruhr that lives exclusively on industry. The Henrichshütte belonging to the Henschel Company was the first target of our concerted efforts in activism.[5] After two years of struggle with deep red Marxism on the one hand and, at least in the earlier days, with the French occupation on the other hand, we managed to hold the town completely in our hands, to push the Marxist front back from its strong position and to plant the flag of National Socialism firmly in the hard soil of Westphalia.

---

[4] Formed in 1921 by Hitler in Munich, the Sturmabteilung (the SA) was a paramilitary wing of the NSDAP; their members were known in English as the Brownshirts, as their brown uniforms resembled those of Mussolini's Blackshirts. They aided Hitler's rise to power but were eventually eclipsed by the Schutzstaffel (the SS) in 1934.
[5] The Henrichshütte Iron and Steel Works was a foundry in the Ruhr belonging to Henschel & Son, a German company that produced transport equipment.

Shortly before I left, we enjoyed the success of making it impossible for the Marxists to hold a rally, even with the involvement of strong reinforcements from out of town. The enemy no longer came to us, so we went to him. The Social Democratic Party no longer dared challenge National Socialism.[6] Instead, they found us ready to answer their questions hand-to-hand.

That had certainly taken a great deal of fighting and gruesome clashes. We neither sought nor provoked this. On the contrary, we were determined to bring our ideology to the Ruhr in peace and without trouble. On the other hand, we understood from experience that when the progress of a new movement is threatened by the terrorism of an adversary, there is no way to get by with fine words or appeals for solidarity and fraternity. We held out an open hand to anyone who wanted to be our friend. But if we were hit with a clenched fist, we only had one remedy: to smash open the fist that was raised against us.

From the outset, the movement in the Ruhr had a strong proletarian character. This was due to the region itself and its people. By its very nature and disposition, the Ruhr is a land of hard work. However, there is a profound and decisive difference between the proletariat of the Ruhr and the average proletariat found elsewhere. The core element of this segment of society is the Westphalians who are still rooted in the soil. The miners who go down into the mines in the early morning are mostly the first- or perhaps the second-generation sons of Westphalian smallholders.

There is still a healthy, natural connection to the soil in this race of people. The International would never have been able to force entry into here if the social conditions of this province had not been truly appalling.[7] However, the wrong that had been committed against the working class here for decades was so unnatural and

---

[6] Since its inception in 1875, the Social Democratic Party of Germany (SPD) has been in thrall to Marxism and more contemporarily socialistic globalism. As such, it is a committed enemy of National Socialism.

[7] "The International" refers to any of three associations founded to promote communist action. The First International was formed by the Jew Karl Marx in London in 1864 as an international working men's association. The Second International was formed in Paris in 1889 to celebrate the hundredth anniversary of the French Revolution and it included a great many Jewish led organizations and Jewish delegates. The Third International, also known as the Comintern, was formed by the Jewish-founded and led Bolsheviks in 1919 to further the cause of world revolution. It was eventually abolished in 1943.

unjust that it inevitably forced those dismayed by it into a movement hostile to the nation and all its supporting institutions.

This is where we began our work. And without our knowingly attaching any importance to it, the struggle to recover the Ruhr proletariat took on a strong socialist character. Socialism, as we understand it, is essentially the result of a healthy sense of justice, combined with a sense of responsibility toward the nation, without consideration for special interests.

Because the enemy used terror tactics, we were forced to defend the movement and drive it forward using fists; thus our struggle took a decidedly revolutionary turn from the start. It is true that the revolutionary character of a movement is determined less by the methods it uses than by the goals it fights for. Here, however, the goals and methods coincided.

This was also reflected in the ideological documents of the movement in the Rhineland and Ruhr. The *Nationalsozialistische Briefe* was founded here in 1925, and in them an attempt was made to clarify the socialist tendencies of our movement.[8] Although we were not theoreticians, nor did we want to be, we had to provide the necessary ideological know-how for our struggle. This soon became a highly sought-after stimulus for further and deeper work for many within the movement in western Germany.

During the years of 1925 and 1926, it became necessary to consolidate the widely branching organizational structures of the movement in the Rhineland and Ruhr. The result of this process was the so-called Gau Ruhr, which had its central office and political seat in Elberfeld.[9] The work in the industrial towns of the west was at first essentially one of activism. At that time, we did not yet have the opportunity to take action in the course of political affairs. The political situation in Germany was so rigid and calcified that this was simply out of the question. In addition, the young movement was still in its infancy, so influencing high politics was not possible.

---

[8] The *Nationalsozialistische Briefe* was a biweekly journal published by the short-lived National Socialist Working Association for approximately one year. This group was founded by Gregor Strasser, while Goebbels was the business manager and chief editor of the journal. The journal's articles focused more on the "socialism" side of National Socialism and would discuss various ideas including class conflict, wealth redistribution, and a possible alliance with the Soviet Union.

[9] A *Gau* was an administrative district used by the NSDAP and eventually the Third Reich.

Activism itself has no fundamental method of its own. It has only one goal; in politics this goal is always to conquer the masses. Any means that serves this goal is good. Likewise, any means that neglects this goal is bad. A theoretical activist who devises an ingenious method at his desk will find himself greatly astonished and upset in the end when that method is not used by a practical activist, or having used it, it does not produce results. The methods of activism are forged by the daily struggle itself. None of us was born to be an activist. We have learned the means and possibilities of effective mass activism from everyday experience and only elevated them to a system through repeated use.

Modern activism is still essentially based on the effect of the spoken word. Revolutionary movements are not made by great writers but by great orators. It is a misconception to assume that the written word has a greater impact because it reaches a larger audience through the daily press. Even though the orator can in most cases only reach not more than a few thousand people with his word—whereas the political writer often finds tens and hundreds of thousands of readers—the spoken word, however, influences not only the person who hears it directly, but it is passed on and carried away by him hundreds and thousands of times. Also, the suggestive power of an effective speech still far outweighs that of a dull leading article.[10]

For that reason, we were mainly and almost exclusively activists in the early stages of the battle for the Rhineland and Ruhr. Mass activism was our only main weapon, and we were all the more compelled to use it as we lacked at the time any weapon in the media.

It was inevitable that the initial successes that we gained in the Ruhr would soon be reflected in the clashes that the movement also had to fight throughout the Reich. At that time, the Party was in a desperate state of affairs shortly after its collapse and despite Adolf Hitler's release from Landsberg Prison.[11] It had made a daring attempt for the ultimate objective and had then been cast down from the greatest heights to the lowest depths. By 1924, the Party was consumed with grueling petty personal quarrels. The sure and steady

---

[10] It is worth remembering that this insight predates the mass consumption of digital media, enabling nearly anyone to reach an audience of millions with any given message.

[11] Landsberg Prison is a penal facility in Landsberg am Lech, a town in southern Germany. It is best known as the prison where Hitler was held in 1924, after the Beer Hall Putsch in Munich (in which the NSDAP led by Hitler attempted and failed a coup), and where he dictated his memoirs *Mein Kampf* to Rudolf Hess.

guiding hand of the man behind bars in Landsberg was missing everywhere.

This all changed after Adolf Hitler was released from prison around Christmas 1924. However, what small and narrow minds had destroyed in a year, a brilliant mind could not rebuild in such a short time. Only shattered remains and ruins could be seen far and wide; despondent and hopelessly resigned, many of the best fighters had turned their backs on the movement and stood down.

Fate largely spared the movement in the Rhineland and Ruhr from this internecine strife. To the extent that it did exist at the time, it was under the pressure of enemy occupation. It was forced to go on the defensive and had to fight for its most primitive existence. It therefore had little time for debates about the Party program, which would have pushed the movement into unoccupied Germany beyond a tolerable limit. Very small, discreetly organized points of support formed its backbone, so long as the enemy remained in the country. Once the French withdrew, these points of support rapidly expanded into powerful local branches with much potential that sought to conquer territory that had long since been taken in the rest of the Reich; it was these local branches where comrades in the struggle engaged in personal and also professional, although very serious and cheerless, disputes.

No one can describe the delightful sense of satisfaction that overcame us all when, despite the difficult sacrifices, we succeeded in giving the movement in the Rhineland and Ruhr a fixed center in Elberfeld by establishing a permanent office. It was still not sophisticated enough to meet the demands of a modern mass organization. But we still had an office, a foothold, a center from which we could venture into the country to achieve our conquests. Soon a finely meshed organizational network spanned over the entire province; this was the very beginning of the Sturmabteilung. Prudent organizers and talented orators assumed command of the local branches, and suddenly new life blossomed from the ruins.

How difficult it must have been for me to give up these promising beginnings and move my activism into an area of operation that I was still entirely unfamiliar with! I had started out here. I thought I had found my permanent home here forever. Only with reluctance could I think of giving up this position and exchanging it for a still vague and uncertain hope of some other success.

*   *   *

All this flashed through my mind again in a muddled and disorderly procession, while the locomotive sped through the gray fog, hissing and howling through the abode of my past work, deeper into Westphalia. What awaits me in Berlin? Today is the ninth of November! A momentous day for Germany itself and especially for our own movement![12] It was three years ago that machine guns rattled at the *Feldherrnhalle* in Munich and the advancing columns of a new Germany were mowed down by reactionaries. Should that be the end? Or is it not rather in our own strength and in our own will that we hope and guarantee that Germany will rise again despite everything and that we will give it a different political vision?

The November evening, oppressive and gray, is already falling over Berlin as the express train chugs into the Potsdam station. Scarcely two hours had passed when I stood for the first time on the stage that would so often become the starting point for our further political growth in the following years. I am speaking to the Party in Berlin.

A Jewish tabloid,[13] which would so often criticize me in later years, was the only publication in the capital of the Reich to take any notice of my first speech: "A certain Mr. Goebbels, who is said to hail from the Ruhr, showed off by spouting the usual clichés."

*   *   *

I was now to take over as leader of the movement in Berlin, which was in a less than pleasant state of affairs at that time. It too had suffered through the trials and tribulations of the entire Party, and like every crisis, this one in Berlin had particularly devastating

---

12 The ninth of November is indeed a momentous day for German history for two reasons. On that day in 1918, Kaiser Wilhelm II of Germany abdicated after the German Revolution, thus marking the beginning of the Weimar Republic. However, Goebbels is here referring to the Beer Hall Putsch in which sixteen NSDAP members were killed, which also ended on this day in 1923.

13 In the German original, the author used the term *Judengazette*. *Gazette* in German is a dated, derogatory term for a newspaper whose journalism is of poor quality. By appending *Juden-* to the front, the author is inextricably linking this substandard journalism to Jews. Although a tabloid is technically only a newspaper half the dimensions of the standard broadsheet, the translator believes the colloquial connotation of "tabloid journalism" provides a suitable context to *Judengazette*.

consequences. Disputes over leadership had shaken the structure of the organization to its core, as far as one could speak of such a thing. For a time, it seemed impossible to enforce order and firm discipline again. Two cliques were bitterly opposed to one another, and neither was able to prevail over the other. The Party leadership had long hesitated to intervene in this chaos. It was correct to assume that, if this situation were to be rectified, reorganizing things in Berlin would have to be done in such a way that it guaranteed at least some stability for the Party for a considerable period of time. Within the Berlin organization, however, there was no reliable leader figure who had the strength to restore the lost discipline and establish new authority. In the end it was decided to transfer me to Berlin for a set period of time with the task of providing the Party again with at least the most basic opportunities to get to work.

This thought first emerged at the 1926 Party rally in the city of Weimar. It was pursued further and took its final form during a shared vacation with Adolf Hitler and Gregor Strasser in Berchtesgaden.[14] I had been to Berlin several times, and during these visits I took the opportunity to study the state of the Berlin organization until I finally decided to take on the difficult and thankless task.

It was the same in Berlin as it is everywhere else when an organization suffers a crisis: knights in shining armor appeared wherever one looked, thinking their time had come. Each gathered a clique or a following around him, with which he tried to gain influence, or if he were the treacherous type, to further the disorder. It was not at all possible to investigate the Party's situation calmly and objectively and reach firm decisions. If the various groups and factions were included in the discussions, we would immediately find ourselves surrounded and besieged by all the coteries and in the end could no longer find a way out.

For a long time I hesitated as to whether I should even take on the unrewarding position, until finally my binding duty convinced me to courageously tackle a job that I knew from the outset would cause me more worry, trouble, and dissatisfaction than it could bring me joy, success, and fulfillment.

The crisis that threatened to break the Berlin movement was essentially of a purely personal nature. There were no differences of

---

[14] Berchtesgaden is a town in southern Germany, in the Bavarian Alps close to the border with Austria. Hitler had been vacationing there since the 1920s, and eventually, during the time of the Third Reich, Hitler had a fortified retreat there.

opinion concerning the Party program or organization. The two groups that were feuding with each other only wanted to put *their* man at the helm of the movement. Thus, there was no other option than to appoint a third party as leader, which neither of the two rivaling factions was apparently capable of doing, at least not without causing serious damage to the Party.

Is it surprising that I, as a newcomer, who did not come from Berlin at all and who only had a very superficial knowledge of the character of this city and its people, was exposed to many kinds of personal and professional resentment from the very beginning? My authority, which at that time was not backed up by any accomplishments, could not be used anywhere to make important decisions. For the time being, the most important thing was to establish such credibility in the first place.

However, at that moment there was no chance of leading the movement to visible political success. What called itself a party in Berlin at that time did not deserve this appellation whatsoever. It was an unruly muddled crowd of a few hundred people with National Socialist views, each of whom had formed his own personal opinion about National Socialism. In most cases, this opinion had very little to do with what is commonly understood by National Socialism. Brawls between the separate groups were the daily agenda. Thank God the media took no notice of this, as the movement itself was, by numbers alone, still so insignificant that even the yellow press, which otherwise leaves nothing unreported about us, passed it by with a contemptuous shrug.

This party was incapable of maneuvering. It could not be used in decisive political action, even disregarding our numbers, simply because of its quality. It first had to be made more uniform, equipped with a shared will, animated with a new burning passion. Its numbers had to be bolstered, and the constrictive dividing lines of party politics had to be forced open. Its name and its purpose had to be drummed into the public mind, and the movement itself had to be fought, if not for love and respect, then at least for hatred and vehement opposition.

The work began with me trying to bring the scattered pieces of the organization together, if nothing else, for at least one group event. A few days after I took over leadership in Berlin, we held our first general assembly in Spandau, where we had the movement's strongest foothold at the time.[15] This event, however, painted the most pathetic picture of the state of affairs within the Berlin movement that had developed during the crisis. The members, who hardly even filled the room, were split into two sides. One side was in favor, while the other was opposed. And since they had fought and raged among themselves to the point of exhaustion, the collective disapproval was directed against me and the new course I had proposed. The troublemakers in the group seemed to faintly sense that it would, however, put an end to all the undisciplined activities in the shortest possible time.

I uttered the words, "The past is behind us, so let us start afresh! Anyone who is unwilling to work with others for this will be expelled from the movement without much ado." As a result, we lost roughly a fifth of the entire Party membership in Berlin in the first instance. Nonetheless, it was my firm belief that the organization, once it was welded together and no longer had any elements that endangered its existence, had in the long run more promise of success, even in terms of numbers, precisely because of its internal unity, than a larger organization that was always and forever menaced by the subversive activities of a handful of professional anarchists.

Many of my best comrades refused to understand that at the time. They believed that we should not go without the handful of members who turned their backs on the Party and threatened it as sworn enemies. Later developments have shown that the movement itself, as soon as it is near the enemy, endures such crises without any danger, and that what we lost in numbers back then was recouped tens and hundreds and thousands of times by a healthy and well-established combat organization.

The Berlin movement already had a permanent head office at that time. However, it was extremely crude. It was situated in some sort of filthy cellar in the rear of a building on Potsdam Street. A so-called secretary lived there with a cash book in which he recorded the daily flow of money as best he could. Piles of documents and newspapers lay in the corners. In the waiting room groups of unemployed Party members debated and passed the time by smoking and fabricating empty rumors.

We called this office the "opium den." And that name actually seemed entirely fitting. It was illuminated with artificial light only, as

---

[15] Spandau is a borough in Berlin and one of its main industrial areas. The NSDAP polled some of its best results in elections in working class districts such as Spandau.

daylight could not reach it. As soon as one opened the door, one was greeted by thick clouds of stale air and smoke from cigars, cigarettes, and pipes. No doubt systematic work of good quality was out of the question here.

The "opium den" (see the ××). First office of the NSDAP in Berlin, 109 Potsdam Street.

The administration of a party must never rely solely on the proper guiding beliefs of its officials. Those beliefs should be a prerequisite that goes without saying for professional work in a party, and therefore does not need to be particularly emphasized. However, those guiding beliefs require something else, and that seemed completely missing in the "opium den": the serious desire and ability to achieve something. It was an utter mess here. There was hardly an organization. Finances were in dire straits. The Berlin branch at the time had little to its name other than debt.

One of the most important responsibilities of the organization was to put the Party on a firm financial foundation and to provide it with the means with which it could take up steady work. We National Socialists take the view that a revolutionary party of struggle, which intends to reduce international capitalism to ruins, must never, ever, be permitted to accept from that same capitalism the funds it needs to expand. It was therefore clear to us from the outset that the nascent movement in Berlin, which I now had the honor of leading, would have to obtain the means for its initial development by itself. If it did not have the desire and ability to do this, then it was not viable, and then it seemed a waste of effort to devote time and labor to a task in which we could have no confidence.

It goes without saying that the management of a movement must operate as frugally as possible. On the other hand, there are certain conditions that must be met for a determined organization; obtaining the necessary finances to ensure this was the object and purpose of my first effort.

I appealed to the willingness of the Party members themselves to make sacrifices. On *Bußtag* in 1926,[16] around six hundred Party members gathered in the Viktoriagarten in Wilmersdorf, in a hall that would later often become the scene of our political triumphs.[17] In a lengthy speech, I explained to them the need for a solid financial basis for the Berlin organization. The result of this meeting was that the Party members agreed to commit fifteen hundred marks every month in donations, with which we were able to give the movement a new headquarters, hire bare-bones administrative staff, and begin the fight for the capital of the Reich.

*   *   *

Up until then, the politics and the people of the city of Berlin had been a complete mystery to me. I only knew it from occasional visits, and even then it always seemed an obscure, mysterious enigma, an enormous city of stone and asphalt that I typically preferred to leave rather than set foot in.

Living there for a few years is the only way one gets to know Berlin. Then suddenly one understands the obscure, mysterious sphinx of a city. Berlin and its residents suffer a worse reputation in the country than they deserve. The blame for this is mostly borne by those nomadic, rootless, international Jews who have nothing to do

---

[16] *Bußtag* is a Protestant holiday in Germany, dedicated as a day of penance and prayer. Eleven days before Advent, it falls in mid-November each year. *Bußtag* in 1926 occurred on November 17th. The author made his appeal on this day of penance likely to underscore the need to make a sacrifice for the greater good of the Party.

[17] The Viktoriagarten was a large hall with a huge beer garden in the Wilmersdorf locality of Berlin. This hall was particularly important because of its use by political organizations of all affiliations. However, for the NSDAP in particular, the "Battle for Berlin" was launched *here* at the Viktoriagarten with Goebbels' lengthy speech. The other "political triumphs" celebrated here include the founding of the National Socialist Schoolchildren's League (a precursor to the Hitler Youth), as well as using Horst Wessel's "blood flag" to consecrate other Party flags.

with Berlin other than eking out a parasitic existence there at the expense of the hard-working native population.

The city of Berlin has an unparalleled intellectual nimbleness. It is lively and energetic and brave; it has less sentiment than reason and more wit than humor. The Berliner is constantly on the go and vigorous. He loves work, and he loves fun. He can dedicate himself to a cause with all the passion of his lively soul, and nowhere is relentless fanaticism, especially in political matters, more at home than in Berlin.

However, this city also has its dangers. Every day the rotary press spews millions of newspaper copies of Jewish venom into the Reich's capital. Berlin is dragged back and forth by a hundred mysterious forces, and it is difficult to gain a firm foothold and maintain a secure intellectual position in this city.

The asphalt provides the ground upon which Berlin evolves and expands at a breathtaking pace. The city does not feed itself from its own supplies, either materially or spiritually. It lives off the farms of the province, but it knows how to return in enticing forms what the province obediently gives it.

Every political movement in Berlin has a fundamentally different character from those in the provinces. There has been a violent fight over German politics in Berlin for decades. This makes the political sort here tougher and crueler than anywhere else.

The pitilessness of this city has also found expression in its people. In Berlin they say, "Take it or leave it!" Anyone who does not get pushy will get lost here.

Berlin needs a spectacle like a fish needs water. This city thrives on it, and any political propaganda that fails to see this will miss its target.

All of Germany's party crises have originated in Berlin, which is understandable. Berlin uses its mind to assess politics, not its heart. However, the mind is subject to a thousand temptations, whereas the heart always beats with the same rhythm.

We only learned to see all of this very late and after many bitter disappointments. But then we based all our efforts on it.

We had now, with great difficulty, brought the finances of the Berlin movement into order and were now able to set about building up the crumbling organization. It was an auspicious moment for us

then, as we did not encounter any resistance from the outside. We were not yet well-known, and to the extent we were known, we were not taken seriously. The name of the Party was still slumbering in anonymity, and none of us had yet managed to make our own name known to a wider audience. This was a good thing, too. This gave us time and opportunity to put the movement on a firm foundation so that, should the fight become unavoidable, it would be able to withstand all attacks and hostilities.

The Berlin SA was already at considerable strength at that time. It traced its glorious tradition, full of fighting spirit, back to the *Frontbann*.[18] The *Frontbann* was the original bearer of National Socialist Party history in Berlin before 1926. However, this tradition had a more sentimental rather than historical character. The SA man, as long as he marched in the *Frontbann*, was a soldier, although the political character was still completely lacking. It was one of the most difficult tasks to transform the SA man into a *political* soldier in the first few weeks. However, this task was made easier by the willing discipline with which the Party's Old Guard, insofar as it marched in the SA, subordinated itself to the new course of the Berlin movement.

---

[18] The *Frontbann* refers to a reorganized and renamed version of the SA. It was formed in April 1924 as a substitute for the SA, which had been banned in the aftermath of the failed Beer Hall Putsch. It was disbanded in February 1925 after the ban on the SA was lifted and was reformed back into the SA.

The SA man wants to fight, and he also has a right to be led into battle. His existence finds its justification only in battle. The SA without a militant tendency is absurd and pointless. When the Berlin SA man realized that we had no other goal than to fight with him for the movement, for the capital of the Reich, he unquestioningly supported our program, and it was mainly due to him that a fresh impetus burst forth so quickly from the movement's chaotic confusion. The Party was then able to fight against its enemies for position after position in a triumphal parade.

It was more difficult back then with a political organization. It had little tradition, and the leadership in most departments was frail, given to compromise, without the strength of morale and will. We had to spend many evenings traveling from one department site to another to erect a solid structure out of the reluctant fragments of the organization. It sometimes happened that one came across local units whose entire behavior was more reminiscent of a patriotic bowling club than a revolutionary fighting movement. Then we had to intervene ruthlessly. A sort of parliamentary democracy had arisen in the political organization, and it was now believed that the new leadership could be turned into the powerless plaything of majority decisions by the various cliques.

This was immediately put to an end. We lost a number of useless elements that had fossilized within the Party. But inwardly they did not belong to us at all.

It was a stroke of luck that the Marxists and the Jewish yellow press did not take us seriously at the time. For instance, if the KPD in Berlin had even suspected what we were and what we wanted, they would have mercilessly and brutally drowned the very beginnings of our work in blood.[19] The fact that people did not even know us at Bülowplatz,[20] or if they did know us, they would smile and walk by, was something our opponents must have often bitterly regretted later. Even if we limited ourselves to consolidating the Party itself and thus directed our effort more inward than outward, this did not seem

---

[19] The KPD was the Communist Party of Germany. There is really nothing to add to this; nonetheless, it should be made clear that the KPD was founded and led by Jews.

[20] Bülowplatz is a public square in central Berlin; it was often the site of mass political demonstrations, especially against National Socialism. In post-war commemorations of those anti-NSDAP demonstrations, it has been renamed numerous times after various communists and to this day is named after the Jewish founder of the KPD, Rosa Luxemburg. This is also the location of the historical headquarters of the KPD.

an end in itself but rather just a means to an end. For us, the Party was not a jewel that we wanted to keep locked away in a precious shrine; rather, it was more like a diamond that we made sharp so that we could later use it mercilessly to cut up the enemy front.

A lot of the fuel for conflict that had been built up within the Berlin movement had already been eliminated when, after a short time, we summoned the leadership of the entire organization to the first *Gau* rally.[21] There the personal problems were conclusively put to an end, and the motto for the entire Party was, "We're starting afresh!"

The flag is planted!

---

[21] The NSDAP rallies held in Nuremberg every year are well-known. However, sub-ordinate units of the NSDAP, such as the Berlin organization's unit, held their own smaller versions of the national rally; these were known as a *Gautag*, which has been translated here as "*Gau* rally."

In Berlin, party crises are unavoidable in the long run. The only question is whether the crises ultimately undermine the party's framework or whether the organization overcomes them. The Berlin movement has been through many crises involving its members, its organization, and its beliefs. Usually they caused no harm but were often, in fact, of great use. In this way, we always had the opportunity to eliminate obsolete useless materials and elements from the organization and to immediately restore the Party's endangered health through a drastic remedy.

This was what happened the very first time. Once the Party had overcome the crisis, it was purged of all miasma and was able to tackle its actual duty with courage and energy.

Then the terror tactics began, although they were felt more in the streets than in the offices. Not an evening went by without our Party members, on their way home, being attacked by red mobs on the street, some being seriously injured. But the organization itself had already become so cohesive that the bloodshed cemented our unity rather than scattering us in fear and anguish.

We could not yet host large-scale combat training as the organization did not have the necessary internal strength to do so. We had to content ourselves with gathering Party members, sympathizers and fellow travelers in small halls,[22] week after week, and dealing in our speeches less with current issues than with explaining the doctrinal foundations of our worldview, hammering them into the heads of our Party members to the point that they could, as it were, repeat it in their sleep. This is how the first nucleus of the party was concentrated into a solid framework. The organization had a foothold, and the ideology was deepened through unflagging political education. Everyone knew what was at stake; the goal had been set, and all our strength could now be brought to bear.

Even back then there were critics: those who criticized every decision from their armchairs and always knew better in theory than we did in practice. We did not care much about them. We figured that our superior achievements would force them to be quiet in the end. We could not do anything without the fellow travelers and know-it-alls criticizing and condemning it. It was the same then as it is today. But the same people who always knew everything before any decision

---

[22] Sympathizers and fellow travelers, in English, are synonymous. However, in German, the word for "fellow traveler" is *Mitläufer*. *Mitläufer* is a derogatory term for a mere supporter of a movement and carries the connotation of being a freeloader.

was made, better than those who bore responsibility for those decisions, were always the ones who claimed to have predicted it, and in the end, they acted as if they had actually made the decision and could then claim success for themselves.

We had ignored them to focus on business. While the small-time critics were at work on us, we worked diligently, often late into the night. We spared no effort and no burden. By fighting hard, we established firm discipline in an organization that was on the verge of anarchy. We waved the flag of our ideology, unmoved by what some people might have said, and sent fanatical men on the march, ready to fight for it unconditionally.

*   *   *

I still remember, with deep emotion, one evening when I, a complete stranger, was sitting on the top of a double-decker bus with some comrades from the *Kampfzeit*,[23] traveling across Berlin to a meeting. The streets and squares of the city were teeming with people: thousands and thousands of people on the move, seemingly with no purpose or destination. Shining above it all was a flickering gleam of light. Then someone anxiously asked whether it would ever be possible to impose the name of the Party, and our own names, onto this city. Even sooner than we could have hoped and believed in those hours, this timid question received an unequivocal answer from the facts themselves.

---

[23] The rise of the NSDAP from 1919 to 1933, when the Party struggled for power, is known as the *Kampfzeit*—literally, "time of struggle".

2. Beginning of Order

The movement in Berlin was now on its feet. The organization was in a satisfactory state despite, for the moment, the extremely low numbers. The financial situation was gradually improving. The Party possessed valuable leadership material in its various organizational elements and was thus able to begin its outward struggle, even if at first only in a subdued manner.

From the outset, it was clear that a new headquarters was essential for the Party. The office where it had been based until now proved insufficient and too primitive. Regular and systematic work was totally impossible there. We therefore quickly began looking for new, more suitable premises. But even these first modest steps taken by the young organization encountered widespread criticism within the Party itself. In any organization there will always be these petty minds; they do not want to and cannot understand that, as the situation evolves, so must the means and methods. When a party is just emerging from the smallest and most humble beginnings, the simplicity of its organization cannot be an end in itself but only a means to an end. A party will be judged solely by how it presents itself to the outside world. The public, most often, has no other opportunity to observe its inner spirit, its cogency, the activity of its supporters, and its leadership. This is why the Party must keep a tight handle on that which is visible to everyone.

The National Socialist movement also had to comply with this principle, especially as it had not entered politics merely to take its share of parliamentary sinecures and ministerial posts, but rather to take the Reich and power by storm. If it was possessed of this daring ambition, then its struggle for power had to take on a form that would allow the outsider too to believe that the Party would indeed achieve its goals in the end.

The last remaining weeks of 1926 were entirely devoted to the Party's internal recovery. There was a great deal to do everywhere. Here, it was necessary to give fresh heart to a timid comrade who had been left breathless by the Party's new dynamic course. There, presumptuous critics had to be put in their place. Elsewhere, it was important to replace the incompetent leaders of a department. The major symptoms of the crisis, only just overcome, were still having devastating effects throughout the entire Party.

We said that a line had to be drawn with the past and that we would start afresh. We could therefore do nothing better than simply pass over in silence all the internal disputes that had occupied many months of the recent past, and give the Party members a new task. Obviously, we encountered a lot of criticism and some hostility in doing so, even within the political leadership. The members of the Party had taken personal quarrels so seriously that they felt they had to fight to the end, without regard for the organization itself. The leadership, on the other hand, believed that this crisis should be considered over and that there were better things to do than engage in these personal squabbles, which led to nothing other than division and driving away the best and most selfless activists.

In October 1926, Hitler sent me to Berlin with the special power to represent him, and I was determined to use this plenipotentiary power uncompromisingly. The Berlin organization had been deprived of firm, unwavering leadership for so long that it had already become quite accustomed to the lack of discipline; naturally, any strict intervention that was not open to compromise was felt to be irksome and presumptuous. I would perhaps not have had all the necessary strength and perseverance if I had not been assured, from the outset, of the absolute confidence of the Party leadership and in particular Hitler himself, as well as their unreserved approval for all my decisions.

Already at the time and very often thereafter, rumors of a personal and political conflict between Hitler and me were spread. There could be no question about such a conflict, either then, today, or ever. I have never entered into politics on my own initiative, and I would not even risk it or attempt it today under any circumstances.

It is not only discipline, which I am convinced alone gives the Party the strength and determination to accomplish something great, that prompted me to it and continues to do so; I feel, moreover, so deeply connected to the Führer since the day I had the great fortune of knowing him as a person and—I dare say—learning to appreciate and love him, both politically and personally. Thus, there will never be an option for me to do anything without his approval, let alone against his will. It is the good fortune of the National Socialist movement that a firm and unshakeable authority was established, as embodied in the person of Adolf Hitler. This ensures that the Party in all its political decisions, sometimes very serious ones, has a secure footing and great resolution. Within the National Socialist community, faith in the Führer is imbued, one might almost say, with an enigmatic mysticism. Apart from the purely psychological value that such a fact represents, it gives the Party itself such formidable strength and political security that it thus effectively stands far above all political organizations and associations.

Adolf Hitler is not only viewed in the Party as its first and supreme Führer; he *really* is. National Socialism against him or even without him is completely unthinkable. He himself rightly pointed out that, in 1919, everyone had the possibility to declare himself against the regime in place and organize a movement to overthrow the tribute system.[24] That he alone was called to this mission and that he also began to fulfill it for all to see is irrefutable evidence that fate had chosen him for this. Only imbeciles and professional rebels can pretend otherwise and act like it is not so. This was never an option for me. Since fate gave me the chance to have not only a political leader but also a personal friend in Hitler, my path was mapped out from the start; today, I can say with deep satisfaction that I have never deviated from this path.

Hitler entered politics as an unknown private. He was not given his name at birth as a gift. Through years of hard and thankless struggle, he imposed his name against the powers of the underworld. From personal experience, he had the deepest and broadest understanding of the political clashes that would now unfold in Berlin as undeniably logical consequences. He was one of the few who always

---

[24] The "tribute system" refers to the so-called reparations Germany owed for the First World War, as imposed by the victors with article 231 of the Treaty of Versailles; for many Germans at the time, the war indemnities represented a national humiliation and constituted blatant theft from the German people.

kept a cool head and nerves of steel in the subsequent crises during the struggle for the capital of the Reich. When the mob of journalists wailed against us, when the movement was the target of bans and persecution, when slander and lies rained down on it, when even the toughest and most steadfast comrades were sometimes dispirited and discouraged, he faithfully stood by us always and everywhere; he led us through our fights and defended our cause with passion even when it was attacked from within our own party; for those fighters on the front line, he always had words of comfort when in danger and words of approval after success—this front line which, progressing despite the most painful sacrifices and the most humble origins, moved against the Marxist enemy.

The more our inexorable advance burst into public view, the more I, too, found myself plucked from the shadows of anonymity and put in the spotlight of public attention. The National Socialist movement represents the principle of personality in its strongest form.[25] It does not blindly adore the masses and numbers, as do democratic and Marxist parties. For us, the mass is merely an unformed substance. It is only in the hands of the artist, whose canvas is the state itself, that a people is born from the mass and a nation from the people.

Men make history! This is our firm belief. Since Bismarck, the German people have lacked men; this is why there has been no great German policy since his passing. The people sense this in a dull and hazy manner. Beginning precisely in the period following 1918, the mind of the masses was filled more and more with the yearning for strong leadership personalities. If democracy fosters the illusion among the masses that the sovereign people want to govern themselves, it is because they were only able to believe it during the short

---

[25] This idea or principle of "personality" is a concept found in National Socialist political philosophy. As Goebbels hints, according to this theory, it takes a "personality" such as Hitler or even Goebbels to organize the masses to become a functional, cohesive unit for the benefit of society, rather than the masses self-organizing within a democracy. One example of National Socialist literature discussing this is *Politische Fibel* (*Political Primer*) by Dr. Hansjörg Männel (Leipzig: Verlag von Theodor Herbert Fritsch, Jr., 1940). In the fifth chapter, "Democracy or Leadership," Männel states, "Against the democratic idea of the *mass* we National Socialists set the idea of *personality*. Everything great in this world, all inventions and all cultural achievements are created by personalities. Our Führer has formed a German folk out of disintegrating mass. Democracy is a symptom of decline in dying peoples (for example, Greece, Rome, and so forth). All ascending peoples are, by contrast, always led by significant personalities" (emphasis in original).

space of time when Germany sank into the fantasy of egalitarianism, as the men who actually governed Germany were not the ideal representatives of the high art of politics. The people only want to govern themselves if the system in power is ill and corrupt. The people feel no desire for either the specific right to vote or a so-called democratic constitution, as long as they are convinced that their leaders are pursuing good and honorable policy. The people simply want to be governed respectably; however, a system that has neither the will nor the capacity to do so then attempts to give the gullible masses a taste for the tempting ideologies of democracy, so as to tranquillize and assuage the rising discontent throughout the country.

The National Socialist movement took the risk of fighting these hypocritical illusions at a time when doing so was widely unpopular. We have opposed the underhanded and irresponsible worship of the masses with the principle of personality. The fact that vigorous, strong-minded characters have gradually emerged within the Party, increasingly representative of the thinking of the entire movement, was only a logical consequence of this conception.

It has nothing to do with "personality." In the hostile press, we have often been criticized for engaging in a sycophancy that is more off-putting than that which existed before the Great War under Wilhelm II. This accusation is totally unfounded. It stems from our opponents' inability to establish comparable authorities in the parliamentary swamp and to instill in the masses a similar confidence in those authorities.

Popularity, when artificially created by the press, usually lasts only a short time; the people endure and tolerate it only reluctantly and against their will. A democratic bigwig who is artificially elevated by the Jewish press to a certain level of popularity, which is already plagued by skepticism, and a true leader of the people who, through struggle and selfless personal sacrifice, wins the trust and unconditional support of the masses are two very different things.

However, it would be overstretching authority if one wanted to always throw one's weight around for every decision that has to be made. The less authority is put into play, the longer it lasts. The intelligent and prudent leader will only rarely use his authority in such a way. On the contrary, he will more often than not endeavor to logically justify to the masses what he does and does not do. Only when persuasion proves to be ineffective or when certain circumstances force him, at least temporarily, to keep the most important and convincing reasons secret will he enforce his decision by reason of authority itself.

Authority is not effective in the long term merely because it is supported and propped up from above, especially when it is increasingly forced to make unpopular decisions and lacks the ability to provide the masses the necessary justification for those decisions. It must always and forever nourish and support itself through its own strength. The greater the achievement that the authority can display, the greater it is itself.

The Party organization in Berlin was pushing for action at a time when the movement was neither capable nor strong enough for it. We opposed this with all our might, even at the cost of temporary unpopularity. Party members had imagined that the appointment of new leadership would mean the start of a full-scale battle. It was not yet understood that certain conditions would have to be met beforehand lest the struggle be abandoned because it was unfeasible to pursue.

To appear before the public with an organization that was not up to the task was out of the question. It was first necessary to consolidate it internally; only then could we begin to conquer Berlin externally.

Every organization rises and falls with its leadership. If it can find a worthy, capable, and prudent leader in some town or province who actively takes charge of the movement, then the party progresses very quickly, even under the most adverse conditions. But if this is not the case, then even the most favorable circumstances will not be able to give it any particular advantage. Therefore, we wanted, first and foremost, to place a well-trained and decisive cadre of officers at the helm of the Berlin organization, and where none existed, to train them for their tasks using the manpower available.

In the early days, our *Gau* rallies, held every month on a Sunday afternoon with ever-increasing attendance, served this purpose. The entire command staff of the organization, both the political and SA leadership, came together at these rallies. The ideological principles of our movement were discussed in doctrinal conferences; the nature of the organization, its activism, and its political tactics were explained and examined from all sides in dialogue. These *Gau* rallies were becoming more significant for the whole organization. They showed the way forward, and the fruits of this concerted educational effort were soon to ripen in the movement's outward political struggle. The character of the Party in Berlin had to be different from that in any other big city or in the countryside. Berlin has a population of roughly four and a half million. This sluggish asphalt monster is tremendously difficult to wake from its lethargic rest. The means used to do so must correspond to the immense size of this city. We can only appeal to millions of people by using language that will also be understood by millions of people.

For the movement, activism in the old Biedermeier style was absolutely not an option.[26] We would have made fools of ourselves, and the Party would never have grown beyond the narrow confines of a sectarian existence. Before the Party's reorganization, the public had only ever regarded us with a certain pity. We were treated as harmless fools, best left to ourselves without causing them trouble.

Nothing could be harder to bear. To be insulted and slandered, to be beaten bloody and thrown in prison—that seemed almost more desirable. But to be looked past with infuriating indifference and at best to be met with a pitying smile would spur on our last reserves of strength; it drove us to constantly devise new methods of public activism, to never miss any opportunity to increase activity to a scale that would eventually take the breath away, if only momentarily, from this giant city: the enemy will laugh no more!

* * *

Methods of activism in Berlin also differ from those in the rest of the Reich. Leaflets, which are frequently used to great effect in the political struggle in the provinces, seem completely unsuited here. Not to mention the fact that we lacked the money to print and disseminate leaflets wholesale to make an impression on this gargantuan city; Berlin is already so inundated with printed material that a leaflet on some street corner is merely accepted out of courtesy, only to end up in the trash the next moment.

Activism through posters and rallies undoubtedly promised better results. However, when used in the same style as the other parties, it would have brought us only marginal success, as the other parties

---

[26] The so-called Biedermeier style refers to specific sociocultural currents prevalent in Germany between 1815 and 1848. This style emerged in tandem with the rise of urbanization and industrialization, which subsequently lead to a burgeoning urban middle class and is consequently closely associated with the bourgeoisie. As a style, it was characterized by restraint, conventionality, and utilitarianism.

were already well-established among the masses. The political camps already formed such an entrenched bloc that it seemed almost impossible to break through them. We had to try to compensate for the lack of finances and staff with imaginative originality, adapted to the mentality of the Berlin population. It was a matter of embodying as much as possible the Berliners' taste for pointed phraseology and compelling arguments. We started early on, and as later developments proved, it was not without success.

Of course, we had to be content for the time being with merely understanding this since we still lacked the means to put it into practice. These issues were the big topic, widely discussed on all sides, at our monthly *Gau* rallies. In the Old Guard of the Party, understanding for these things was particularly keen and vivid. We only occasionally found a defeatist or carping critic who would vent his bile on these projects, but the majority of the Party members collaborated with good heart and had only one desire: to get the organization up and running as quickly as possible in order to begin practical work.

As this preliminary work was beginning, I was very fortunate to find a number of friends and comrades who not only showed the broadest understanding of my plans, but still seemed disposed, in terms of character and ability, to give visual life to what I was trying to achieve by speaking and writing.

In this vein, I cannot fail to mention a man who, from the first day of my work in Berlin until today, has been at my side in everything with courage and selfless motives and whose divinely gifted artistry provided him the talent to chart new paths for the Party and its artistic style, which was then vague and barely formulated. This is our graphic artist Mjölnir,[27] who at the time had just completed his first series of National Socialist posters and was now swept into a movement that was boldly storming forward thanks to the Berlin organization's renewed activism. He was the first—and only—to give a graphic representation of the typical SA man, through a series of posters that captivated the masses.

The SA man will remain abidingly in the imagination of future generations as Mjölnir cast him with his pencil onto paper, or with his brush onto canvas with passionate inspiration. It was in fact the beginning of a new artistic style for which the young movement

---

[27] Hans Schweitzer, who went by the pseudonym Mjölnir (Thor's hammer), was an artist who produced many illustrations for the NSDAP, including the drawings found in this book.

unconsciously longed and by which it spontaneously found, in a simple, grand, and even monumental way, its first form of animated and stirring expression.

This young artist has the rare talent of mastering with brilliant virtuosity, not only illustrated representation, but also compelling formulation of words. For him, the image and the slogan are born from the same unique intuition, and the two together then create a thrilling and rebellious mass impact from which neither friend nor foe can flee in the long run.

In this respect too, I have learned a lot since I started working in Berlin. I had arrived from the provinces and was still suffused with their ideas. For me at the time, the masses were just an obscure monster, and I had not yet possessed the will to conquer and master them. Without such a will, tenacity is useless in Berlin. From a sociological point of view, Berlin is a conglomeration of masses; if anyone wants to become someone and be important here, he must speak the language of the masses, to organize and justify their actions so that they can muster sympathy and devotion for him.

I inevitably developed a completely new style of political discourse due to these early observations. If I compare today the transcripts of my speeches before Berlin to those of my later speeches, the former seem almost tame and prosaic to me. And the same goes for all the activists in the Berlin movement. The rhythm of a city of four million souls pulses, like a burning breath, through the empty rhetoric of the many propagandists in the Reich's capital. Here, a new and modern language was spoken which no longer has anything to do with archaic and so-called *völkisch* forms of expression. National Socialist activism was tailored to the masses. The Party's modern conception of life sought and found here a modern and rousing style.

Alongside the *Gau* rallies, our mass meetings took place week after week. These were most often held in the large hall of the Kriegervereinshaus,[28] which took on almost historical significance for the movement's future. Only to a limited extent could they truly be described as "mass" meetings. The masses were only represented there in exceptional cases. The listeners, around one thousand to fifteen hundred men and women, were recruited mainly from Party comrades from all districts of Berlin, with a few fellow travelers and sympathizers. For the moment, it suited us perfectly. We thus had the

---

[28] The Kriegervereinshaus was a large building in central Berlin used by numerous veterans' associations and would become a preferred meeting place for the NSDAP.

opportunity to fully express ourselves among one another, without running the risk of being immediately distracted from the subject by a confusing and threatening debate with political adversaries. There we familiarized the rank-and-file members of the Party with the fundamental ideas of National Socialism, which were sometimes only understood in a very vague and confused manner. There we fused them to the unified system of a political worldview. We later realized the enormous importance of this work that we would carry out systematically week after week. If, subsequently, the Party itself and its Old Guard in particular were invulnerable to all outside attacks, if each crisis confronting the movement was overcome without difficulty, it was because the members of the Party had been trained with integrated and firm dogma; thus, they were ready to foil all the traps into which the enemy wanted to lure them.

Here should be mentioned the other contributions that the Old Guard made in developing the Berlin movement. There were in fact only a few hundred of them, a small sect that was ridiculed for gathering around our flag. They were exposed to all the slanders and persecution, and yet they drew from their own humiliation the courage to grow beyond their strength. The first National Socialists in Berlin did not have an easy life. Anyone who declared his support for us not only had to face the terror of brute force, he also had to suffer, day after day, in the offices and workshops the icy disdain and smiling contempt of the indifferent masses, full of presumptuous arrogance. Usually, the rank-and-file member suffers much more from this than the one at the head of the organization. He is always the first point of contact with the opponent; he is his neighbor at the workbench and at the office desk. He sits next to him on the bus, the streetcar, the subway. It was already a recklessly daring feat to conspicuously wear even just our Party badge or to be seen with one of our newspapers in public.

But that is not enough. As long as the rank-and-file member is convinced that there is a mass organization behind him, that his cause is in good hands, that victory after victory and triumph after triumph will be achieved by his movement, then humiliation, disdain and smiling contempt are endured with a silent pride. However, this was not the case at all back then. Far from it; we were a laughably inconsequential association. Nobody even knew our names. We were regarded as somewhat narrow-minded dissidents. Not only had the movement been unsuccessful, but setbacks and failures compounded its dire existence.

Besides this, it must also be noted that the several hundred Party comrades had to make incredible and almost unbearable sacrifices for the young, growing movement. We know that it is much more difficult to get a business going than to keep it running. The most basic foundations of our organization had to be laid. All this cost a lot of money, and this money had to be raised from the meager pittance of ordinary people.

We perhaps would often have despaired of our task at the time, had it not been for the admirable dedication of our comrades to the common cause, never shying away from sacrifice, which constantly filled us with new courage and faith. Today, new Party members sometimes find it too much to pay the regular monthly dues, which in most cases are quite tolerable. In those days, every Party member gladly sacrificed ten percent, if not more, of his income for the Party. Because we started with the belief that, if we gave ten percent of our income to the present system under the compulsion of the law,[29] we had to be prepared to sacrifice at least as much out of moral duty for a Party we believed and hoped would restore honor to the German nation and bread to the German people.

The Party's Old Guard still forms the backbone of the entire movement. The comrades of that time can be found everywhere, at every level of the organization. Even today, as then, they quietly and discreetly do their duty. This one as department leader, and that other as SA leader; this one a street cell leader, and that other a cell operations foreman; and many, as in the old days, as simple Party members or as little-known SA men. Their names do not go down in history, and they have come to terms with that. But as Party guards who clutched and waved our flag when it threatened to waver and fall, they will be remembered forever, so long as National Socialism is spoken of in Germany.

We formed this Party guard into a small, strictly disciplined organization. This organization was called the Freiheitsbund.[30] Its name alone expressed that its members were prepared to sacrifice

---

[29] This refers to taxation in Weimar Germany.

[30] The Freiheitsbund, or "Freedom Alliance" in English, was specifically intended as a network of approximately two hundred Party members who, in addition to their ordinary obligations to the NSDAP, pledged increased monthly dues to provide it with a firmer financial footing.

everything for freedom. They met every month for a whole year, and with the spirit of heroic self-sacrifice, in addition to risking life and limb, put at the Party's disposal the financial means it needed to get going.

Forward, Berlin!

Spandau was at that time one of the first strongholds of the SA's political organization. It is said that someone from Spandau is baptized with water different from the Berliner's. Indeed, this area had some challenging peculiarities. But when it came down to it, when the Party needed fighters, whether to defend itself or expand its positions on the attack, this stronghold stood up like a single man. It was from this district that we fought the initial battles of the Berlin movement. The first National Socialist mass meetings that caused a sensation in the capital were held in Spandau. From there, the movement progressed, growing inexorably toward Berlin itself.

Even today, when one of the Old Guard comes man-to-man and in private criticizes this or that defect within the Party, it brings deep satisfaction. We know from the outset that this criticism is out of concern for the good of the Party, and that the man who makes it in no way wants to be self-important; on the contrary, he is only acting in the best interest of the Party. The same man, who, in private, brings up real or perceived faults, would rather hold his tongue than damage the Party with rash public remarks. Through his years of activism and having proven that he is ready to sacrifice himself completely for the Party if necessary, he has earned the right to bring forward criticism.

What a pitiful effect, in comparison, those critics and loud mouths have who only appear at the moment of victory, who feel obliged, above all, to diminish the success of others with their criticism, a success that was accomplished without them and sometimes even despite them. Back then, when all we had to do was work and fight, when everyone had to pull his weight, these snivelers did not stick around. They made us do most of the work. It was only when the wagon was out of the rut, so to speak, that they appeared at the periphery of the Party with their brilliant advice and bourgeois platitudes.

Spandau SA

As for me, a modest Old Guard with a proven track record, who has been fulfilling his binding duty to the movement for years, without claiming fame or honor for it, even if he is not as eloquent as those crafty rhetoricians, is a hundred times preferable to those bourgeois cowards who suddenly discover a warm heart for us today when the movement has become the biggest party in Germany.

*　　*　　*

On January 1st, 1927, we said goodbye to the "opium den" on Potsdam Street and moved to our new premises on Lützow Street. By today's standards, even the new office still seems relatively small, modest, and rudimentary, as do the working methods that were introduced there. But at the time, it was a risky leap. We climbed out of the cellar and made it to the ground floor. The smoke-filled waiting room was transformed into a true organized political headquarters. The movement could be judiciously managed there. In addition, the new office now offered the possibility of admitting and incorporating more members into the Party and its organization. The bare essentials of personnel had been hired, although sometimes after bitter arguments with the Party members themselves who had already become so accustomed to the old routine that they considered it indispensable, and thought that any movement away from it was a symptom of capitalist boasting and craving for status.

Our goals were ambitious, but in the end events moved much more quickly than even our lofty plans for new heights could. The triumphal progress of the movement had begun and would soon become unstoppable. As our success increased, the masses trusted us more and more. The Party saw its membership grow.

In this new office, the Party had a solid base in which we could work, organize, and hold much-needed meetings. It ensured a calm and orderly course of business. From here, new working methods were introduced into the movement. The management itself gave the organization the strength to march inexorably forward and to continuously progress.

*   *   *

During those weeks, Wolfgang Goetz's play *Neidhardt von Gneisenau* was performed several hundred times on a Berlin stage with great success.[31] It was my first major theatrical event in the Reich's capital. I will never forget the sentence uttered by this lonely general who did not understand the world and whom the world did not understand: "May God give you a goal, no matter what it is!"

---

[31] *Neidhardt von Gneisenau* was originally released in 1922, and it came to enjoy wide popularity and success several years after its initial release. The play followed the military career of August Neidhardt von Gneisenau, a Prussian general who successfully defended Kolberg from Napoleon's forces in 1807.

God gave us a goal, but what it was did matter. We believed in something. We understood the goal, and it was our unshakeable faith that we would achieve it. And so, full of courage and self-confidence, we set off, unaware of the worries and distress, the terror and persecution that lay ahead

44 Lützow Street (see the ✕✕).
Second office of the NSDAP in Berlin

3. Terror and Opposition

If a political movement is weak in numbers and it lacks rigor in its campaigning and activism, then it remains, regardless of its objectives, ignored by its enemies. But as soon as it passes a certain stage in its development and begins to occupy public thought, its enemies are forced to deal with it. As they had until that point disregarded our existence and this was beginning to harm them, they sought to make up for lost time with an excess of hatred, lies, slander, and violent terror.

In politics, it is not just the ideals one defends that are pivotal, but also—and to a decisive extent—the means of action one is willing and able to employ in defense of those ideals. An ideal without action will always remain a theory, no matter how correct it is. Thus its proponents must concentrate all of their political rigor on conquering power and then implementing the ideal through the use of that power.

After we had rebuilt the internal structures of the organization in two months, the National Socialist movement had now passed the first stage of its development. It was consolidated and could now be launched into the fight. But to the same extent that its organization was perfected and its activism began to take its first tentative steps outward, the enemy was beginning to notice. He quickly recognized that it would not be prudent to ignore us any further, although the movement was still in its initial, rudimentary stage. The Party had already established itself in certain positions of power. Its worldview was clarified, and the organization firmly anchored. It was thus difficult to oust it from the positions it had quietly assumed.

Marxism, as is well known, seeks to deceive the public into believing that it has ineradicable control over the Reich's capital. As soon as it was aware of our intentions and understood that we had no other aim than to put an end to the slogan "Berlin, forever red," which actually still rung true at the time, Marxism launched the full force of its organizations against our movement. The counteroffensive, unleashed against us across the board, was not waged by communists alone. For once, the Social Democrats and Bolsheviks were in complete agreement, so we had to defend ourselves on two fronts: against the Bolsheviks, who dominated the streets, and against the Social Democrats, who held the public offices with an iron fist.

The struggle began with lies and slander. As if by command, all the parties dumped the nastiest demagogy onto our young movement. The Marxists wanted to prevent its doubting followers from attending our rallies, which were becoming increasingly popular. Instead, they gave a misleading image of us, falsified in the most shameful and untruthful way. Our movement was portrayed as a crowd of criminal, rootless elements, its supporters as hired thugs, and its leaders as vicious, vile agitators who, in the service of capitalism, had no other task than to sow the seeds of discord among the ranks of the Marxist workers' front, which wanted to abolish the bourgeoisie.

So began a virulent hate campaign on an unprecedented scale. Hardly a day passed without the newspapers reporting on atrocities committed by National Socialists. Most of the time, *Vorwärts* or *Die Rote Fahne* set the tone,[32] and then the whole orchestra of the Jewish press finished off the furious symphony with wild demagogy.

At the same time, the red terror and bloodshed raged in the streets. On their way back from meetings, our comrades were stabbed or shot in the dead of night. They were ambushed ten, even twenty, to one in the courtyards of tenement blocks. They were threatened even in their own meager abodes, and it was typically a waste of time when we sought police protection.

We were used to being treated as second-class citizens, worthless provocateurs, and slanderers who deserved nothing better than to be

---

[32] *Vorwärts* is a newspaper published by the SPD. *Die Rote Fahne* was another far-left newspaper that vacillated in its political alignment from Social Democrat to communist to Spartacist.

stabbed in the back with the dagger of brotherly love by some sinister creature from the proletarian suburbs.

This time was difficult and almost unbearable for us. But despite all these bloody sacrifices forced upon us, this fight also had its good sides. We could no longer be ignored or passed over with icy contempt. We had to be named, even if it was with seething reluctance. The Party made itself known. Suddenly it found itself at the center of public interest. Like a raging tempest, it had swept away the lethargic calm of political Berlin, and now everyone had to state his opinion regarding it: yes or no. What seemed to us at first an enticing yet unattainable desire suddenly became reality. People talked about us. We were discussed, and the public did not fail to ask more and more about who exactly we were and what we wanted.

The journalists had thus achieved something that was certainly not their intention. It would have taken us years of work and effort to achieve the same: the movement was no longer unknown. It had a name, and where it was unwelcome, it was treated with open contempt. Until now, people had barely smiled at us. Two months of work was enough to make the enemy stop snickering. The harmless game became deadly serious. Our opponents made a number of psychological blunders. By persecuting our leaders and ordinary activists in the same manner, they merely united the two in a common front of ardent resistance. Had they spared the leadership to go after the men alone, our situation would have been untenable in the long run, as it would inevitably have triggered a wave of instability and discontent in our own ranks. By acting as they did, they for better or worse helped to cement camaraderie within our desperate group and to make our movement so united that it was subsequently able to withstand all aggression.

Police and court summonses then suddenly piled up on my desk—and not because I had somehow instantly become a worse citizen, but seek, and ye shall find, as it were. If someone has made the decision to take up the fight against the regime in power, then he will soon hardly be able to take a step without breaking one law or another.

After a number of those casual invitations, I soon had to make my way to Moabit,[33] where I appeared for the first time in Berlin's spacious, communist courthouse, in which I would later make many guest appearances. Here, I learned to my great surprise that I had been guilty of high treason. I was rigorously interrogated and soon realized that not a word I had written or spoken had escaped the notice of the senior authorities.

The real public battle began in our strongest base, Spandau. In the last days of January 1927, we held our first mass meeting there, which could rightfully be called a mass meeting. We had made an appeal to the Marxist troops, and it did not go unheeded. More than five hundred shock troops from the Roter Frontkämpferbund were interspersed among our listeners throughout the hall.[34] There was soon to be complete pandemonium. They obviously were not there to listen to what we had to say. Rather, as they say in their slang, they wanted to beat the meeting to a pulp.

Their admirable intention was thwarted by the masterly tactics we used during the meeting. We explained from the outset that we welcomed open discussion with anyone in good faith, that each party would be allotted ample time to speak, that the rules of procedure for the meeting were of course set by us, the hosts, and that anyone who failed to observe the rules would be promptly ejected by the SA.

It was a language that, in Berlin, had previously only been spoken at Marxist rallies. The leftist parties felt overconfident in their strength and made light of the non-Marxist associations that presented elegant debates against Marxism. They laughed it off and did not bother to attend such rallies.

---

[33] Situated in central Berlin, Moabit is a neighborhood hosting the city's central criminal court and its accompanying jail facilities.
[34] The Roter Frontkämpferbund (RFB) was a far-left paramilitary group associated with the KPD during the Weimar Republic.

Right from the start, things were different with us. We spoke a language that Marxists also understood, and we came to discuss issues of the utmost interest to the common man.

The proletarian has a highly developed and keen sense of justice. Whoever knows how to seize this will always be assured of his sympathy. We announced our desire for dialogue, and we put ourselves on a level with the proletarian, man-to-man. This way, from the outset, the Marxist provocateurs would not be able to sabotage the meeting before it even began with their unscrupulous demagoguery. That was good enough for us, because we knew that if we managed to speak to these misguided, anxious people at all, then we would have already won.

For this first workers' rally, the presentation lasted more than two hours. Its subject was socialism, and during my speech, I was delighted to see that these five hundred men who had come to cause trouble with their proletarian fists, as *Die Rote Fahne* wrote, had become calmer and calmer. At first some paid agitators did try to disturb the sedate progress of the meeting with clever disruptions, but they soon fell silent one after the other, when faced with the icy disapproval of their own comrades. In the end, the solemn silence of collective attention pervaded the whole assembly.

The meeting began. A Marxist agitator had climbed onto the stage and was just about to stir up a fight with empty rhetoric when alarming news arrived from outside: Marxist shock troops had attacked, beaten, and stabbed two of our Party members on their way home. One had to be taken to the hospital with life-threatening injuries. I immediately stood up, informed the audience of this horrific incident and declared that the NSDAP could not allow the representative of a party, whose cowardly followers were trying in the darkness outside to replace with violence what they clearly seemed to lack in intelligent arguments, to speak at one of our meetings.

The description of the depraved and vile ambush having intensely outraged the whole assembly, the remaining communists, likely seized by a guilty conscience, began to fall silent. The categorical announcement that the NSDAP refused to be involved with them aroused the thunderously enthusiastic approval of all those listening in good faith. The Marxist provocateur stammered a few more words of protest before he was snatched from the stage and thrown out, despite that not being our intention.

In my closing remarks, I stated once again with firmness and clarity that we were always and everywhere ready to speak man-to-man with any political activist in good faith, especially with an honest worker. However, any attempt to oppose us with bloodthirsty terror would be met with the same violence. If they use their fists, then so should we.

The meeting ended in victory all around. The Marxist hooligans withdrew in silence with their tails between their legs. That evening our comrades were filled with a sense of comfort for the first time, knowing that the movement in Berlin had now grown beyond the narrow confines of a partisan sect; the fight was on, and we were now all on the front line. There was no going back. We had challenged our adversary, and everyone knew that he would not let this challenge go unanswered.

Indeed, the following day the reaction of the Marxist press came. We already knew that those liars on Bülowplatz and Linden Street would misrepresent the truth as the exact opposite. We would be pilloried as cowardly provocateurs and murderers of workers who beat harmless proletarians to a pulp because they had asked for a political discussion.

With big, bold headlines, the Marxist journalists screamed in the Reich's capital: "The Nazis cause a bloodbath in Spandau! This is a wake-up call for all revolutionary workers in the Reich's capital!"

And below was this unequivocal threat:

"They will pay dearly for this!"

We now had only two possibilities left: either we could give in and cause the Party to forfeit its reputation with the proletariat once and for all, or else we could strike again with double the force and challenge the Marxists, on our own initiative, to a new debate. We knew this decision would be critical for the fate of the movement.

We had posters printed to cover the walls of Berlin:

The bourgeois state is coming to an end! We must forge a new Germany! Intellectuals and laborers, the fate of the German people is in your hands!
    On Friday, February 11, 1927, at the Pharus Hall.[35]
    On the topic:
    "The Collapse of the Bourgeois State. . . "

---

[35] The Pharus Hall was a meeting hall in Berlin's Wedding district, and it served as the usual venue for KPD events.

*　　　*　　　*

It was obviously a provocation the likes of which Berlin had never before seen. Marxists considered it arrogant for a nationalist to openly express his opinions in a working-class district. And in Wedding of all places?![36] Red Wedding belongs to the proletariat! It has been that way for decades, and no one found the courage to oppose it and prove otherwise.

Pharus Hall

And the Pharus Hall? That was the undisputed domain of the KPD. Here, it held its Party congresses. Here, it gathered its most loyal and active members almost every week. Here, the empty phrases of world revolution and international class solidarity had been regurgitated time and again. And that was exactly where the NSDAP decided to hold its next mass meeting.

It was an open declaration of war. That is what we meant, and that is what the enemy understood. Our Party members were enthused. Everything was on the line. The fate of the Berlin movement now boldly hanged in the balance. It was win or lose!

The decisive day, February 11th, 1927, was approaching. The communist press was overflowing with bloodthirsty threats. We would not expect a warm reception, as they would not want us to

---

[36] At the time of this event, Wedding was a working-class district and communist stronghold in central Berlin.

return. At the unemployment offices, it was openly announced that we would be beaten to a pulp that evening.

At the time, we had no idea of the danger we were about to face. Even I did not yet know the Marxists well enough to foresee in detail the possible consequences. I dismissively glanced through the empty yet gloomy rhetoric of the red press and awaited the decisive evening eagerly.

"The Bourgeois State is Coming to an End!"

"As it should! Because it is no longer able to secure Germany's freedom, a new Germany must be forged… A Germany of work and discipline! History has chosen you, the intellectuals and the laborers, for this task! The fate of the German people is in your hands! Never forget! We must act now!"

Around eight o'clock in the evening, we drove to Wedding in an old, run-down car. A cold, gray mist drizzled down from the dark sky. Our hearts were bursting with anticipation.

As we drove down Müller Street, we realized that tonight was not going to be smooth sailing. Groups of shady characters were lurking at every corner. It was clear that they wanted to teach our members a hard lesson before they even got to the meeting.

In front of the Pharus Hall stood dark crowds of people, venting their fury and hatred with loud, threatening insults.

The head of our protection service made his way toward us.[37] He quickly informed us that the meeting hall had been completely full since 7:15 P.M. and had been closed by the police. He reported that two thirds of the audience was RFB militants. This was what we wanted. A decision had to be made here, one way or the other. We were prepared to give it our all.

As we entered the room, we were hit by a stifling odor of beer and tobacco. The room was very hot and humid. A great clamor of voices roared through the hall. The audience was seated, piled on top of each other, making it difficult for us to walk toward the stage.

No sooner had I been recognized than a hundred howls of fury and vengeance rang in my ears. "Bloodthirsty dog! Murderer!" Those were the more friendly names we were called. But the fervent ovation given by our own Party members drowned out their insults. From the stage rang out loud battle cries. I realized at once that we might be the minority tonight, but this minority was determined to fight and would triumph.

In those days, it was still our custom to have an SA leader chair the Party's public meetings. That was the case here. Tremendously tall, he stood up front and called for silence by raising his arm. That was easier said than done. A burst of scornful laughter was the reply. Insults flew from every corner of the room. There was growling and screaming and roaring. Scattered throughout the crowd were drunken Marxist revolutionaries who had found their courage for this evening at the bottom of a bottle. It was impossible to calm the room down. The class-conscious proletariat had obviously not come to debate but to fight, to break things, to put an end to the fascist nightmare with the calloused fists of workers.

We did not misunderstand it for even a moment. We also knew that if we succeeded this time, if our adversary failed to destroy us as he had threatened, then the movement's march to future victory in Berlin would be unstoppable.

About fifteen to twenty SA and SS men stood courageously in front of the stage, in full uniform: a bold and brazen provocation for any Marxist militant! Behind me on the stage stood a hand-picked group of the most reliable men, ready at a moment's notice to fend

---

[37] The protection service was the Schutzstaffel (SS for short; meaning "Protection Squad"). At the time of this event, the SS was a small battalion within the SA charged with maintaining order at Party demonstrations. Leading the Berlin division at the time was Kurt Daluege.

off the onslaught of red thugs with force, if necessary, even at the risk of their own lives.

The communists had made an obvious tactical error. They had isolated some of their small groups throughout the entire hall, but the rest were clustered in one corner of the room. Here, I immediately realized, was the center of trouble. Action would have to be first taken there—and ruthlessly. Every time the chairman tried to open the meeting, an unknown individual would stand on a chair and screech, "Point of order!" in a mocking tone. Then the others would loudly chant the same phrase hundreds of times over.

If we take from the masses the one who leads them or even the one who incites them, they become masterless and easily controlled. We therefore had, at all costs, to silence this cowardly agitator who thought he was safe surrounded by his comrades. We tried a few times to do so peacefully. The chairman would shout amid the growing din in a voice already hoarse, "We can argue after the presentation! But we determine the rules of procedure!"

These efforts remained unsuccessful. With his incessant interruptions, this troublemaker only wanted to create disorder in the meeting and ultimately bring things to a boiling point. Then a violent skirmish would naturally ensue.

As our efforts to peacefully restore order to the meeting had proven fruitless, I called the head of the SS aside. Immediately his men moved in dispersed groups through the raucous crowd of communists. The RFB militants were surprised and stunned, and before they realized it, our comrades had taken the provocateur down from his chair and led him through the frenzied rabble onto the stage. It was not over yet, and what I had been waiting for happened just as quickly. A mug of beer was hurled through the air and crashed to the ground; that gave the signal for what would be the first major battle in a meeting hall.

Chairs were broken, legs torn from tables, glasses and bottles were brought out like cannons in a matter of seconds. And off it went. For ten minutes the battle raged back and forth. Glasses, bottles, table and chair legs whistled indiscriminately through the air. The noise was deafening. The red beast had been unleashed and now wanted its prey.

It seemed at first we were hopelessly lost. The communist attack had started so spontaneously and so violently that it took us completely by surprise, even though we had been prepared for it. But barely had the SA and SS men, who were spread throughout the hall and in front of the stage, recovered from their initial astonishment, when they counterattacked with bold courage. Then it became quite clear that, although communism really does have the masses behind it, as soon as they come up against a disciplined and determined adversary, they become cowards and flee. In the blink of an eye, those red scoundrels that had come to sabotage our meeting were driven from the room. The peace that could not be made with goodwill was restored with force.

Berlin SA leader Kurt Daluege (+) and his adjutant.

During a violent brawl, one is often barely aware of its different stages. They are only recognized later. To this day, I have an image imprinted on my mind that I will never forget: this young SA man, unknown to me until then, was standing on the stage. To protect the leadership, he was throwing projectiles at the oncoming red mob. Then suddenly he was hit in the head by a beer glass thrown from a distance. Blood began pouring from his temples. He collapsed to the ground yelling. After a moment he stood up, grabbed a jug of water from the table, and threw it with a sweeping motion into the room where it shattered on the head of an opponent.

The face of this young man remains fixed in me. It was etched eternally in my memory during this episode which happened in only a flash. This SA man, gravely wounded at the Pharus Hall, would soon become my most reliable and most faithful comrade, and he has remained so ever since.[38]

Only after the Marxists had retreated from the battlefield, screaming and cursing, could we see how heavy the losses were. Ten of our men lay bleeding on the stage, most with injuries to the head, and two with severe concussions. The table and stairs leading to the stage were covered in blood. The whole room was an expanse of rubble.

And in this wasteland of blood and ruins suddenly stood our towering SA leader. He resumed his post and declared with iron calm, "The meeting shall continue. The speaker has the floor."

Neither before nor since have I spoken under such dramatic circumstances. Behind me, groaning in pain and soaked in blood, our severely wounded SA comrades—all around me, debris, broken chair legs, shattered beer mugs, and more blood. The whole assembly froze in icy silence.

At the time, we lacked a trained medical corps, which is why we were obliged, finding ourselves in a proletarian suburb, to have our gravely wounded members transported by workers from the ASB.[39] Right outside the meeting hall were scenes that were frankly beyond description in their disgusting cruelty. These savagely depraved men, supposedly fighting for the brotherhood of mankind, insulted our pitiful, defenseless, and seriously injured members, attacking them with remarks like, "Isn't that bastard dead yet?"

It was impossible to give a coherent speech under such conditions. I had barely begun before a team of medics entered the room again to remove more severely wounded SA men on stretchers. One of them, whom these brutal "apostles of humanity" inundated with the most obscene and odious jeers, called out to me in desperation. I

---

[38] The name of this SA man was Albert Tonak, who would eventually become Goebbels' chauffeur.
[39] The ASB is the Arbeiter-Samariter-Bund, a German aid agency focused on providing medical care. While it is officially politically and religiously unaffiliated, it has close historical connections to the labor movement in Germany and the SPD.

stopped my speech, cut across the room and the few remaining communist thugs—who, by the way, stood aside timidly and silently—and said goodbye to my injured SA comrade.

I spoke of the unknown SA man for the first time at the end of my speech.

An amusing incident allowed this bloody clash to end on a somewhat positive note. After the address, when the floor was called to discussion, some miserable oaf came forward, stating that he was a member of the Young German Order.[40] With a burst of pastoral emotion, he implored everyone to seek fraternity and civil peace; he passionately lamented the immoral futility of this bloodshed and declared that only profound unity makes us strong. After a deep bow to the audience, he was about to begin reading a patriotic poem to complete his high-minded nonsense when a straightforward SA man made the entire assembly erupt in laughter after saying, "Shut up, you little weakling!"

*   *   *

The battle in the Pharus Hall concluded with this amusing interlude. Outside the police had cleared the street. The SA and SS were free to go. A decisive day in the history of the National Socialist movement in Berlin had ended.

No words can describe the flood of lies that swept through the Jewish press the following day. The communist riff-raff, whose entire political existence consists in inciting fratricide, suddenly wanted to play the harmless victim and accuse our movement of murdering workers when all it had done was defend its right to life.

Below are a few extracts from the press concerning the incident: *Berliner Morgenpost*,[41] dated February 12th, 1927:

At the Pharus Hall, at 142 Müller Street, last evening around nine o'clock, a serious brawl broke out between communists and members of the German Socialist Worker's Party, who

---

[40] The Young German Order (Jungdeutscher Orden) was a right-wing nationalist organization in Weimar Germany.

[41] *Berliner Morgenpost* was (and remains today) a daily newspaper with headquarters in Berlin. It was founded in 1898 by the Jewish newspaper proprietor Leopold Ullstein.

were holding a meeting there.[42] There were numerous casualties. Four individuals were taken to Virchow Hospital by ambulance, while the remaining ten or so were treated on site.

The German Socialist Workers' Party held a political rally last night at the Pharus Hall, in the northern part of Berlin. Several hundred communists had gathered in front of the meeting venue, and a large number of them had entered the hall. Heckling from the audience was non-stop. Suddenly there was a large uproar, which quickly devolved into a brawl. The parties attacked each other with chairs, beer glasses, and other objects. The venue's interior was wrecked. A large police presence eventually separated the fighters and made a number of arrests.

Die Welt am Abend,[43] dated February 12th, 1927:

Yesterday evening, violent clashes broke out in the Wedding district between National Socialist agents provocateurs and police on the one hand, and workers from Wedding on the other. The National Socialist Workers' Party had convened a meeting at the Pharus Hall, where a certain Dr. Goebbels was to give a lecture on the collapse of the bourgeois state. The meeting, with an estimated two thousand attendees including numerous communists and Social Democrats, was turbulent from the start.

The National Socialists had set their sights on provoking them from the outset. The chairman of the meeting, Kurt Daluege, declared, "There is no arguing against us," as the communists came forward. Loud protests immediately erupted, leading to the brutal intervention of a security force of some three hundred men wearing swastikas. Violent brawls ensued. The fascists beat the workers with chair legs and beer mugs. During the clash, several workers were seriously injured. The communist and Social Democratic workers were

---

[42] "German Socialist Workers' Party" is a clumsy portmanteau of the DSP (German Socialist Party) and the NSDAP (National Socialist German Workers' Party). The DSP was a right-wing party within the German *völkisch* movement founded after the First World War and was eventually subsumed into the NSDAP in 1922.

[43] *Die Welt am Abend* was a Berlin-based communist tabloid during the Weimar era.

finally pushed into the street by those wearing swastikas, where a huge crowd had gathered.

After police arrived, they tried to clear Müller Street on both sides, intervening harshly against the workers. Further violence ensued, particularly on Amrumer Street, where a total of seventeen arrests were made.

The events in and around the Pharus Hall spread throughout the neighborhood like wildfire. New groups of workers constantly arrived, the outrage directed especially against Hitler's security services which maintained an aggressive attitude.

Police tried to keep the crowd back, and reinforcements arrived to escort the swastika-clad men to the Putlitz Street train station. At the corner of Torf Street and Trist Street, there were further clashes. Police claim that stones were thrown at them. In any case, the cops fired a large number of shots. Twenty new arrests were made, and the suspects taken to the police headquarters.

But the unrest did not end there. At the corner of Nordufer Street and Lynar Street, further violence broke out when, here, too, retreating swastika-wearing men attacked the workers. Six people were seriously injured here, in addition to the thirty identified so far who have been slightly injured.

Die Rote Fahne,[44] dated February 12th, 1927:

National Socialists Attack Workers: Premeditated Assault at the Pharus Hall!

"Yesterday evening, a meeting of National Socialists took place at the Pharus Hall, as announced by public notice. Hence, many workers attended, and the room was full. The subject of the meeting, which was the decadence of capitalism, explains why a worker rose at the start of the meeting asking to speak on a point of order to request discussion. The chairman of the meeting then declared that there would be no discussion during this meeting. This was the signal for the National Socialists to launch an outrageous and malicious attack.

---

[44] As its name implies ("The Red Banner"), *Die Rote Fahne* was a German newspaper affiliated with the far left.

Troops of thugs, specially recruited from Schöneberg,[45] had piled up a large quantity of chairs and beer mugs in the gallery before the meeting, so this was a well-prepared assault. Just as the chairman refused to speak on the point of order, the National Socialists began bombarding the workers downstairs with chairs and beer mugs from the gallery. Violent clashes ensued. Many workers were injured, some very seriously. There were even reports of deaths, but this has not yet been confirmed.

News of the National Socialist attack spread like lightning through Wedding, where workers took to the streets and staged huge protests against the National Socialist murderers. Although the police came down hard on the workers, new groups continued to form.

We protest in the strongest terms against these cowardly, murderous attacks. Workers, unite against the fascist murderers!

Such was the response of the Judeo-communist press to a defeat so unexpected that, at first, it seemed to have completely lost its mind.

We soon and often afterward shoved the term "murderer of workers" down their own throats. We refused to stay silent. We tried to show the public, during years of struggle for the truth, where the real murderers of workers must be sought and found.

The fact that we were now called "bandits" was, for us, coming from the mouths of the Jews in the Karl Liebknecht House, nothing more than a title of honor.[46] And when they referred to me as the "chief bandit," we picked it up more quickly than they had expected; it soon became a famous nickname in our own ranks, not only in Berlin but throughout the Reich.

In one fell swoop, the solid leadership authority we had lacked in our Berlin organization had been built up and consolidated by these successes. A combative movement must be led into battle; if the rank-and-file member sees that the leadership is making progress in its struggle, not only in theory but also in practice, he will quickly gain

---

[45] Schöneberg is a locality in Berlin.
[46] The Central Committee of the German Communist Party, made up overwhelmingly of Jews, had its seat in the Karl Liebknecht House. It was named in honor of Karl Liebknecht, the German communist leader who was summarily executed in the aftermath of the failed Spartacist uprising in January 1919.

confidence in it and follow it unconditionally. The leadership, for its part, gains the ability to use its burgeoning authority in all critical decisions. And so it was with us. The Berlin movement now had a central focus. It could no longer be artificially divided by disagreements. In its leadership and in its base, there was coordination and commitment to one another, and thus the movement became capable of maneuvering major political actions. At the time, we were unable to gauge the full extent of this gain. It was to serve us well in later years, at times when the movement was exposed to the harshest trials and when we needed to give it a solid base and a secure, infallible course at decisive moments.

*   *   *

At that time I also made my first contact with the so-called intellectual spokesmen of nationalism. But I must admit that their acquaintance did not satisfy me very much. Among these literary champions of our cause, I found barely one who showed the slightest trace of understanding of the struggle for nationalism across the proletarian neighborhoods. On the contrary, they met in intellectual circles, where they dissected the nationalist worldview into a hundred thousand atoms and then painstakingly and artificially pieced them together again. They indulged in mental gymnastics, brilliantly reflecting their inventors in their own mirrors, but which did not provide any kind of consolation or encouragement to the fighting nationalist front, this front which stood outside their smoke-filled meeting rooms, bloodied and ready for sacrifice.

Nationalism is a matter of deeds, not words. The intellectual champions of this cause must beware of languishing in academic discussions. We are not here to emulate the pretentious style of the Jewish intelligentsia and their dazzling verbal fireworks. Nationalism can use these methods in times of emergency as needed, but they must never become an end in themselves.

The National Socialist movement became great through its speakers, not its journalists. If one of them took up the pen, he did so only to put it at the service of the organization. With these nationalist writers, on the other hand, I mostly had the impression that they wanted to put our organization at the service of their pens. That was my verdict on them from the start. Above all, they seemed to lack the necessary courage in their convictions. They were afraid of displeasing the so-called elites of "social literature." It is a common fear among intellectual philistines, who dare not protest against any Jewish insanity for fear of appearing outdated and being ridiculed.[47]

Campaigning from a truck

Nationalism was always decried as reactionary politics by social elitists. It is therefore necessary to have the moral courage to shout it in the faces of the scavengers in the newsrooms: if in their opinion nationalism is reactionary, then in God's name we are reactionaries. But we are in no way prepared to allow our worldview to be dictated to us by some boastfully arrogant pencil pusher.

Nor should anyone believe he impresses the men of Jewish literature by trying to rival their panache of words or finesse of style. In the end, power itself is what they respect, and they only lower their voices when a fist is brandished in their face.

*   *   *

To our delight, the Battle for Berlin and its demand for blood began to increasingly attract the interest of the whole movement. It was a sigh of relief throughout the whole Reich. What had previously been considered impossible and absurd—to seek out the enemy in

---

[47] An "intellectual philistine" (*Bildungsphilister* in German) is a concept in Nietzschean philosophy. It refers to an individual who believes himself to be educated and cultured but in reality is not. One of the key characteristics of this sort of individual, according to Nietzsche, is the opinion that public education ought to focus on vocational training rather than studies of the humanities or liberal arts.

his own lair and challenge him to a fight—was now becoming reality. The movement throughout the Reich supported us. From every corner of the country, we received donations of money for the wounded SA men of Berlin. This enabled us to give them at least the minimal necessary protection and care. The front-line activists were given the reassuring affirmation that behind them stood a great movement, pursuing their cause with a fiery beating heart.

Cottbus, 1927

The movement was underway. In a long convoy of trucks, the Berlin SA set off toward the provinces. One parade followed the other. A National Socialist day of freedom was celebrated in Cottbus, which culminated in an aggressive police crackdown.[48] In Berlin, one meeting followed another. We challenged the KPD to a fight once again. Four days after the battle in the Pharus Hall, we called for another mass demonstration in Spandau. Once again, *Die Rote Fahne* lashed out, palpitating with indignation, and declared that we must be ended once and for all.

But it was far too late now! The dam had broken. The Berlin SA occupied the room down to the last man. It did the RFB no good to spread their shock troops throughout the streets. A few timid members of our Party may have tried to persuade me to stop provoking

---

[48] Cottbus is an industrial city, on the Spree River, approximately eighty miles from Berlin. The first major rally of the National Socialists in Cottbus was the so-called day of freedom, which left a total of seventeen individuals injured in the ensuing clashes with trade-union agitators.

the already agitated KPD, at least for the time being, but those attempts were all in vain.

In six cars we drove up Heer Street from Berlin, as we had learned that scattered RFB groups wanted to keep us out. We had set up our headquarters in a quiet restaurant in the woods behind Spandau, and from there we sneaked back into the city. The KPD was unable to wreck our meeting, as it had intended. After the meeting had ended, there was a bloody shoot-out with them on Putlitz Street, which left a few of us seriously wounded, but we were victorious nonetheless.

* * *

The attempt to drown the young National Socialist movement in its own blood, this movement that was breaking through in the heart of Marxist strongholds, had failed across the board. We had learned a lot during this struggle. The united front of international Jewry, which we had long recognized, had once again formed against us. Anyone who compared the *Berliner Tageblatt* with *Die Rote Fahne* in those days could hardly tell the difference.[49] Both papers saw us as a menace to society. Both felt their power threatened by us. Both called the police on us. Both were trying to prod the state authorities against us, who had to intervene to save the day, since their terror tactics seemed to have failed.

The movement had gone through its baptism of fire. It did not hesitate to seek out the enemy in his own lair, to force him to fight, to do battle in valiant desperation.

SA man! This title, before then still completely ignored and unknown in Berlin, was now suddenly surrounded by a halo of glory and mystery. Friends pronounced the words with admiration, and enemies with fear and animus. The daringly zealous spirit of this troop quickly won them status and prestige. They had proven by their action that somebody can fight for a cause despite the most adverse circumstances, if behind it lies political passion, strong courage, and smirking contempt. Terror, to the extent it was used against us, was broken. The reputation of invincibility had been stripped from Bolshevism, and the slogan "Berlin, forever red," was rejected and became obsolete.

---

[49] The *Berliner Tageblatt* was a liberal, although not necessarily socialist, daily newspaper in Berlin. As a reminder, *Die Rote Fahne* was a far-left publication closely associated with socialism and communism.

This became our starting point. In the face of the bloodshed and terror unleashed against us, we were ready to resist. It would not be long before this front of resistance, which was defending its first positions, launched a political attack across the board!

Advertisement for the second mass meeting in Spandau.

4. The Unknown SA Man

The unknown SA man! This term, given for the first time to the public at the Pharus Hall after a bloody battle, spread like wildfire through the movement. It was the vivid expression of that political soldier in combat who had stood behind National Socialism in the face of the threat lingering over the German people.

At the time, there were only a few thousand people throughout the Reich, and particularly in Berlin, who took the bold step of wearing the brown shirt and thus branding themselves as political pariahs.[50] But these few thousand men had decisively paved the way for the movement. It is due to them that the SA's first beginnings were not drowned in blood.

Later, it was disputed whether "SA" was an abbreviation for Sportabteilung or Sturmabteilung.[51] But it did not matter, because the abbreviation had already become a concept in itself. It forever evokes the type of political soldier by whom the new Germany was first represented in the National Socialist movement.

---

[50] The SA wore a distinctive uniform that was commonly identified by its brown shirt. Thus, they were also known as the Brownshirts.

[51] Before 1921, the group that would eventually become the SA did not have an official name and in many cases no formal structure or organization either; it was merely a group of Party members with the goal of protecting Party meetings from leftist attacks and interruptions. In August 1921, Hitler was calling it the Sportabteilung or "Sports Division," perhaps in an attempt to legitimize it in the eyes of the authorities. However, a few months later, in November 1921, it would officially assume the title Sturmabteilung or "Storm Division."

The SA man cannot be compared at all with a member of any other paramilitary formation. These latter organizations, in essence, are apolitical, patriotic at best, but always devoid of clear political objectives. Today, however, patriotism is a matter we have to move beyond. There was no forerunner of the SA man in the old Germany. He arose from the violent political forces after the war. It was not, and is not, his task to offer shuttle service to money-grubbers or to guard bourgeois cash boxes like security guards and factory watchmen. The SA man was born of politics and thus is destined, once and for all, for politics.

He differs from ordinary Party members by taking upon himself a greater number of certain duties for the movement, especially that of protecting it when it comes up against brute force and breaking the terror directed against it. It is well known that Marxism has grown through terror. It took over the streets using terrorism, and because no one in the bourgeois parties opposed it, it dominated the streets until the emergence of the National Socialist movement. The bourgeoisie considered it uncouth and undignified to take to the streets, to demonstrate for and advocate a political ideology.

But today modern politics is played out in the streets. Whoever can conquer the streets can also conquer the masses and thus conquer the state. In the long run, only the display of force and discipline will win over the common man. A just ideology, championed with the right means and implemented with the necessary energy, will always ultimately win over the broad masses.

The SA man represents the clear and popular strength of the National Socialist movement to the whole world. When people attack it, he defends it by any means. That was of course easier said than done at that time, because Marxism claimed to be the only one in charge and considered it a challenge when another opinion even dared show itself. Over time, the bourgeois parties, like cowards, had submitted to this arrogance and raised not even the slightest objection. They had given way to Marxism and were content with defending the unstable positions of liberal democracy in parliament and in trade associations.[52] In doing so, they lost every form of defiance,

---

[52] Not to be confused with a trade union, a trade association is a special interest group founded and funded by businesses within a specific industry. Their primary purpose is to promote and advocate for the common interests of its member companies, typically by lobbying for favorable government policies.

and Marxism had no difficulty in overthrowing them with bold mass vigor, putting them on the defensive once and for all.

As is well known, the best defense is a good offense. And if the defense is carried out in a weak, half-hearted attempt, as is the case with the bourgeoisie, the adversary will rapidly conquer position after position, until he violently forces the defender out of his last entrenchments.

Such had been the situation in the Reich since the revolution of 1918. In Berlin, even more so, this situation had fossilized into an automatically accepted state of affairs. It seemed the Marxist parties alone had the right to claim the streets for themselves. At every opportunity, they appealed to the masses, and by the tens and hundreds of thousands they marched to the Lustgarten in a display of their might and undiminished strength to the public.[53]

We understood that National Socialism could never conquer the masses if it did not also assert its right to the streets and boldly wrest it away from Marxism. We knew this would involve bloody battles. The public offices, which were for the most part in the hands of Social Democrats, were in no way willing to use the state's power to guarantee equal rights for all citizens, as the constitution would have required.

We were therefore forced to provide ourselves with the protection that the state refused us. We constantly needed to guarantee that our public action remained undisturbed, which necessitated a special defensive unit, because Marxism very quickly recognized in National Socialism its only serious and viable opponent. It also knew that in the long run National Socialism would be capable of prying from it the proletarian masses who were still marching behind the international ideology of class, and integrating them into a newly formed nationalist, socialist front.

The SA was born of all these considerations. It suited the natural need of the National Socialist movement for protection, and the SA man was its political soldier. He declared himself ready to defend his worldview by any means, and if necessary, to respond to violence with violence.

---

[53] The Lustgarten is a park in central Berlin. During the years of the Weimar system, it was the frequent site of large political demonstrations and rallies for communists and socialists.

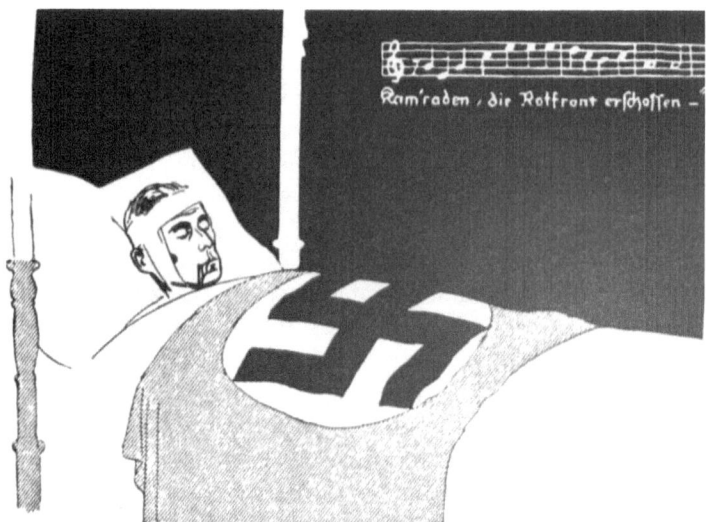

Horst Wessel! A dead man calls to action!

The emphasis here is on the political side. The SA man is a *political* soldier. He serves a political function. He is not a mercenary or a henchman. He believes in what he defends and what he stands up for.

The SA is part of the overall framework of the National Socialist movement. It is the backbone of the Party. The movement will stand and fall with it.

Certain elements that joined the movement later have attempted to falsify this conception. They wanted to unyoke the SA from the overall Party, to create an independent unit which would only make itself available to the Party in case of necessity, at the discretion of its own leaders. This is the exact opposite of the idea that led to the birth of the SA. It is not the Party that comes from the SA, but the SA that comes from the Party. It is not the SA that determines the policy of the Party, but the Party that determines the policy of the SA. Pursuing politics in private, or even attempting to dictate the political course to Party leadership, cannot and must not be tolerated within the SA. Party officials set Party policy. The SA has the task of advocating for the implementation of that policy.

This is why it is necessary that the SA man be taught and educated, as soon as possible, about the worldview that he serves. He must not thoughtlessly stand up for something that he does not understand at all. He must know what he is fighting for, because it is only through this knowledge that he will find the strength to devote himself entirely to his cause.

The Jewish newspapers in particular persecuted the SA with incomparable hatred. Since there could be no serious doubt that the SA served the National Socialist worldview with blind fanaticism and a heroic spirit of self-sacrifice, the yellow press attempted to attribute this attitude to false and insincere motives. They tried to make people believe that the SA man was nothing more than a hired thug, a mercenary, ready to risk his life for money. The conception of the medieval mercenary, it was said, was resurrected in the SA, and in the end, the SA man only pledges allegiance to those who promise and provide him with the best rations and the highest pay.

Disloyal elements had crept into the National Socialist movement, and for a time occupied some of the highest command posts in the SA and actually encouraged these unscrupulous lies.[54] They tried to trigger a rift between the Party and the SA, and they always rationalized their treacherous and worthless goals with the financial claims and demands of the SA. Public opinion would thus frequently conclude that the SA man was being paid by the Party for his service and that the National Socialist movement controlled a troop of reckless, hired mercenaries who were prepared to do anything and everything. That idea could not be further from the truth. Not only is the SA man *not* paid for his service to the Party (even if that service is dangerous and sometimes bloody), but he must also make tremendous material sacrifices. Especially in times of heightened political tension, he looks after the movement every evening and sometimes entire nights, whether it is protecting a meeting, putting up posters, distributing flyers, recruiting members, collecting subscriptions for the newspaper, transferring a speaker to his venue, or escorting him home. It is not uncommon for some SA men to sleep in the same clothes for weeks on end during particularly intense election cycles. At six o'clock in the evening, they start their work for the entire night. When they are done with that duty, they are back to work an hour or two later at the factory or office.

Such political heroism did not deserve accusations of being for sale. Besides, it is simply impossible to find someone willing to push

---

[54] This may be a possible reference to Walter Stennes, the former leader of the Berlin SA, who led the so-called Stennes revolt in 1930 and was ultimately expelled from the NSDAP that same year.

the spirit of self-sacrifice so far for the sake of money alone. People want to live for money, but rarely do they want to die for it.

The leadership of the National Socialist Party did the only right thing by ruthlessly removing the elements that gave the SA the stigma of being mercenaries, as they caused the worst possible injury to the movement. They are to blame for the fact that today any writer thinks he is entitled to slander the brave political soldiers of our movement as hired thugs.

We knew very little about all this at a time when the idea of the SA was just beginning to take root in the Reich's capital. The political leadership had called for a fight, and the SA had responded immediately by placing itself at its disposal. Of course, the SA was the actual moving force behind the decisive clashes that were to lead beyond repression and persecution to the glorious rise of the movement in the capital of the Reich.

*   *   *

The SA wears a uniform: a brown shirt and a brown cap. Some, therefore, assumed that the SA would be a military unit. That is wrong. The SA is not armed and is not trained for military action. It serves political purposes using political methods. It has nothing to do with the numerous paramilitary organizations, mostly emerging from the Freikorps.[55] These paramilitary units generally have their roots in the old Germany. The SA, on the other hand, is the embodiment of the new Germany. It is consciously political. Politics is its meaning, its goal, and its purpose.

The National Socialist movement also formed its own political brigade, most active in the SA. It was able to rely on it for all its political activities, thus gaining a considerable advantage over the other parties, who must devote substantial financial resources to all their campaigns. For this same reason, the Party leadership was often subsequently criticized for having reduced the movement's revolutionary forces to bourgeois advertising. These criticisms fail to understand the very essence of propaganda. A modern political struggle must be fought with modern political methods, and the most modern

---

[55] The Freikorps were irregular units of troops composed of German volunteers, originally fighting in the First World War. After the war had ended, they became involved more domestically and often fought against Marxists and communist partisans.

of all political methods is propaganda. At the same time, it is the most dangerous weapon that a political movement can use. There are ways to combat any political tactic, but the effects of propaganda are irremediable. If, for example, a follower of Marxism is shaken even for a moment in his faith, he loses confidence in Marxism; he is, so to speak, already defeated, because he lost his active resistance at that very moment. What he no longer believes in, he no longer defends from attacks, let alone starts a fight for it.

When the SA engages in propaganda, it is merely employing a modern political tool. This in no way contradicts its original purpose, nor does it run counter to the goal for which it fights.

It has also often been said that the work of modern propaganda contradicts the Prussian military spirit, the last champion of which is the National Socialist SA. It would have been to the advantage of the old Prussia to use the weapon of political propaganda more often and with more resolve than it did. The old Prussia only tried to persuade the world with its achievements. But what good is the finest achievement if it is reviled and denigrated abroad, if lies undermine all the hard work and talent that went into it? We in particular experienced this during the war, to the great misfortune of the German nation. Our engineers developed defenses against all the weapons that the enemy invented and used against us. We had gas masks and anti-aircraft guns. What we lacked was international propaganda organized on a large scale by the state, capable of standing up to the Entente's campaign of shameless lies. We were left defenseless against the inflammatory propaganda of the enemy coalition. For years, these poor Belgian children, whose "hands had been chopped off by German soldiers," were shown abroad, or the supposed atrocities of German officers were depicted in film, theater, and the press to an emotional audience over and over.[56] In this mass psychosis, American finance was able to prod the United States into war, and

---

[56] The British propaganda against the German Empire, especially during the time of the First World War, was extensive and pervasive. Although this anti-German sentiment dates to well before 1914, it greatly intensified that year with the British entry into the First World War. A month after the United Kingdom entered the war, a lie began circulating that German soldiers had planned, coordinated, and carried out a massacre of the civilian population in Belgium, including murder, rape, mutilation of children, looting, arson, and indiscriminate destruction. The fear of Germany was so intense and irrational that, for example, the Royal Kennel Club of the United Kingdom actually renamed German shepherds as an entire breed to "Alsatians" to avoid using the word "German."

the enemy coalition was able to convince its soldiers that they were going into combat to defend civilization and humanity, and to fight against barbarity and the impending destruction of culture itself.

When the National Socialist movement takes into account the bitter consequences of the German side's disastrous sins of omission, it only proves that the movement is far from reactionary, and that it does not blindly worship the past merely because it is the past. The SA's training to employ the weapon of propaganda ruthlessly in no way detracts from its fighting spirit. Propaganda is simply a new form of expression for modern political warfare, as it has become necessary with the advent of Marxism and the organization of the proletarian masses.

But better than any theoretical exposition is the success that proves we were right to use this tool. Hearing the howls of fury from Marxism, we quickly noticed that our massive propaganda was bothering it and inflicting ghastly injuries on its organizations.

Obviously, the Marxist parties did not take it lying down. They organized their defense, and as they had no intellectual arguments to oppose our logical, well-reasoned political argument, they resorted to brute force. Our movement was threatened by a bloodthirsty terror that has not abated to this day but has in fact worsened week after week, month after month. Especially at that time, when the Party in Berlin was still in its infancy, the SA, as part of the active struggle of our movement, had to endure the worst. Because he wore the brown shirt, the SA man was already branded as fair game for attack. He was beaten bloody in the streets and chased wherever he dared show his face. To even attend a meeting he would have to risk his life. Every night, Marxists attacked our comrades, and the hospitals were soon full of grievously injured SA men. One had his eye gouged out, another had his skull fractured, and a third lay with a bullet in his abdomen. This heroic bloodletting, suffered in silence, had made inroads into the ranks of the Berlin SA. And the more firmly we planted our revolutionary banner in the asphalt of the Reich's capital, the greater and more unbearable became the sacrifices that the organization as a whole, and the SA in particular, had to make.

We cannot be blamed for glorifying this heroic struggle and crowning the SA man with the halo of brave political activism. Only in this way could we give him the courage to adamantly persevere. And we never tired of showing our comrades that they were devoting themselves to a great cause, worthy of their enormous sacrifices.

From time to time, the Berlin SA would leave Berlin on a freezing winter Sunday. They would march in tight columns through the snow and rain, through the remote villages and towns of Berlin's surrounding regions, to recruit for and promote the National Socialist movement.

If we were refused accommodations in a village, a barn was quickly cleared out at the home of a sympathizer. Our speakers would then address the amazed villagers. And we never left a village without first establishing a solid base for the Party.

It was at this time that our graphic artist Mjölnir composed his lively series of SA men in combat: six postcards with passionate graphics, artistic testimonies of the bloody combat that we were waging for the capital of the Reich. We remember the now famous charcoal drawing of a wounded SA man, with this caption: "Never forget! Berlin SA!" It galvanized the entire movement. All eyes were focused on the heroic efforts of the Berlin SA. The struggle for the Reich's capital suddenly became popular all over the country. The movement throughout the Reich followed the breathtaking progress of the Party in Berlin with anxious hearts.

"Our flag flies in the sky." This catchy slogan, appearing on one of the six postcards, was now justified. Despite the terror and persecution, we had now firmly and unshakably planted the flag of the National Socialist ideal on our soil, and never again—this was our inviolable resolution—would it be brought down.

*   *   *

It was very difficult to house our wounded comrades, to care for them and watch over them as they healed. In Berlin's mainly urban public hospitals, the junior staff was heavily infiltrated by Marxists. We had cruel experiences there with our wounded. The care was very poor most of the time, and many comrades felt abandoned by both God and man in the hands of a socialist nurse or a Jewish doctor. Some of our most intrepid self-starters had their heads, so to speak, constantly wrapped in bandages. It was not uncommon for the same SA man to be injured three, four, or five times in the span of a couple of months, ending up in the hospital each time. We first tried to get out of the situation by sheltering our wounded in a makeshift infirmary and providing them with the bare minimum of medical attention from our own resources, mostly thanks to the donations that came from all corners of the Reich.

The SA was then, and probably still is, mainly composed of pro-letarian elements. Among these, the unemployed formed the main contingent.[57] By nature, the worker is not content just to believe in a political ideal, but he is ready to fight for it. The worker is destitute, and he who is destitute is always more prepared to risk everything for a cause. He has, in fact, nothing to lose but his chains; this is why he is capable of fighting for his political convictions with much more devotion and fervor than the bourgeois. The bourgeois fall prey to more scruples. His upbringing and education prevent him from committing to a political ideal with the same unhesitating passion.

Soon, the SA developed a strong tradition full of fighting spirit. The SA man had a tough battle ahead of him, but he was justifiably proud of the fact that he could stand up for the Party. To belong to the SA was to belong to the elite of the entire movement.

"From the grave we march on!" One of Mjölnir's drawings.

---

[57] This was written during the height of the Great Depression.

"An alley for freedom!" One of Mjölnir's drawings.

"Never forget the Berlin SA!" One of Mjölnir's drawings.

The true strength of the SA lies in the fact that it is essentially made up of proletarian elements. It is due to this fact that the SA, and with it the entire National Socialist movement, will never drift into the waters of bourgeois compromise. The proletarian element, especially the SA, constantly provides the movement with that unbroken revolutionary impetus, which it has happily retained to this day. Many parties and organizations have sprung up since the end of the war, and after a brief rise, have sunk back into the bourgeois swamp. Compromise has infected them all. With the revolutionary activity of its SA men, the National Socialist movement had the guarantee that its fighting spirit would remain intact and that the great political passion of its early days would endure.

Through the spirit and character of the SA, a very particular lifestyle and demeanor developed over the years. The SA man is a new political type, and as such, he has also created in his language and in his attitude an external mode of expression that corresponds to his inner nature. The spirit of camaraderie, which imbues all levels of the SA, is worthy of admiration and sets an example for the entire Party. Proletariat and bourgeois, farmers and city dwellers, young and old, rich and poor—all merge in the SA to march as a united bloc. Distinctions of class and rank disappear. All serve a shared ideal, and the brown uniform is the expression of the same basic conviction. The university student extends his hand to the apprentice, and the prince marches alongside the peasant's son. Risk and sacrifice are borne in common, and anyone who excludes himself from the spirit of this valiant camaraderie no longer has a place in the SA. Positions of leadership are acquired by merit, and they must be earned anew every day through exemplary bravery.

The language of SA is hardy and in touch with the people. They are on familiar terms with one another. This is where the new front of the national community is being formed, which, we hope, will be the trendsetting example of a German nation organized on a new basis.

In March 1927, we finally had to risk organizing the first parade in the capital of the Reich. One Saturday evening, the SA gathered in Trebbin for its first major *Märkertag*.[58] Near a mill, a gigantic pile of wood was set ablaze, and under a night sky strewn with stars, the

---

[58] Trebbin is a town approximately twenty-two miles southwest of Berlin. The *Märkertag* was a short-lived recurring event in Brandenburg, the area surrounding Berlin. It was celebrated by the SA mostly for propaganda and recruitment purposes.

Berlin SA took an oath never to abandon anything in the shared cause, and to continue to defend it, no matter how severe and menacing the dangers may be. Sunday was filled with large SA rallies in Trebbin itself, and then the units left by train for the Lichterfelde-Ost train station, from which the parade toward West Berlin was to set off in the evening. None of us suspected that this rally would result in such serious and fatal bloodshed.

An unfortunate coincidence meant that on the same train as the SA men leaving Trebbin for Lichterfelde-Ost there were large groups of the RFB militants, who were returning from a political rally in Leuna.[59] The political police, which is usually so eager to monitor National Socialists and scrutinize our speeches in the hope of finding any incriminating evidence, was criminally negligent that day by allowing the most polarized political opponents to board the same train for a nearly hour-long journey. Given the tense political atmosphere in Berlin, violent clashes were inevitable. As soon as they boarded the train at Trebbin, the SA men were fired upon by the RFB militants in a cowardly ambush; during the journey, a small-scale war with fatal consequences broke out, culminating in an open shootout on arrival at the Lichterfelde-Ost station.

I had left Trebbin by car with a few comrades without even an inkling of these events so as to prepare for the safe transportation of the SA men to the Lichterfelde-Ost station. In front of the station, a huge crowd of people was already waiting for the SA men to arrive so they could accompany a parade through western Berlin.

Just before the train arrived, the Spandau SA, which had left Trebbin in trucks, reached the square in front of the station and lined up nearby for the start of the parade. The train pulled into the station, and while the sympathizers waiting outside were still watching for the SA to arrive, gunfire erupted on the station platforms not knowing exactly what was happening from outside. Shortly after, a seriously injured SA comrade was carried out of the station, and the horrified crowd learned that the moment the train left the SA came under heavy fire from RFB militants, who continued their journey to the Anhalter train station, clearly thinking they would be completely safe in their compartments. At that same moment, a dauntless SA man

---

[59] Leuna is a small industrial town in eastern Germany, approximately one hundred miles southwest of Trebbin.

*This is how red murder works! / **"Murder!"** / 'Five hundred of these marauders attacked twenty-three red soldiers. . . . The murderers look like this. [Illustration of an SA man.]"*

jumped onto a car of the departing train, pulled the emergency brake and brought the train to a stop.

An SA leader was lying on the platform shot in the stomach; others had been hit in the legs or pelvis. The SA units were extremely outraged and wanted revenge on their would-be assassins. As fate would have it, one of the RFB militants was a member of the *Landtag*.[60] Thus, this time, not only the corrupted but also one of the corrupters are held to account by their victims. It was very difficult to hold back the frenzied crowd and prevent them from letting the worst happen. Amid the clamor of anger and indignation, the communists left the station under police protection. After a few minutes, order returned to the SA groups, the procession assembled for departure, and shortly after moved silently and grimly through this dark part of the city, toward the west of Berlin.

---

[60] A *Landtag* is the parliament of a *Land* in Germany, in other words, a state- or province-level legislature.

It was the first time that the streets of the Reich's capital resounded with the marching footsteps of SA battalions; they were perfectly aware of the magnitude of the moment. Through Lichterfelde, Steglitz, and Wilmersdorf, the procession emerged at rush hour in the middle of the Jewish metropolis at Wittenbergplatz.[61]

A little later in the evening, some particularly insolent Hebrews who could not keep their filthy mouths shut received a few slaps to the face, which provided the Jewish press with the opportunity it was hoping for to relaunch its unrestrained smear campaign the next day. These journalists surpassed themselves in their rage and wild slander. The *Berliner Tageblatt* was already alluding to a pogrom. Mention of the "innocent passer-by who looked Jewish" appeared for the first time in the columns of the capitalist press—this innocent passer-by who the public was led to believe had been attacked by callous brutes, only because he looked Jewish. Tear-jerking eyewitness reports filled the columns of the panicked Jewish press. People called for self-defense, they shouted, threatened, and created an uproar, they appealed to the police and the state, they impetuously demanded that the shameless behavior of the swastika zealots no longer be tolerated. It was declared that the capital of the Reich was not Munich, that it was necessary to resist our movement from the outset. What was happening here in the streets, they said, was no longer politics; rather, it was organized crime, and the criminals must be made to feel the full force of the law. *Die Rote Fahne* and the capitalist newspapers were now intimate friends. Jewish interests were threatened, and the political differences, which were artificially established between the two sides, conveniently disappeared. In trembling indignation, all Israel demanded," Enough is enough! Ban them!"

Difficult days lay ahead. The fate of the movement hung by a thread. To be or not to be, that was the question. This time, however, an outright ban could still be avoided. But we now knew that we had grown ripe for a ban, and we were convinced that it would be enforced against us at the first opportunity.

On the other hand, we firmly believed that the movement had become so strong that it would ultimately triumph over all resistance, including intimidation tactics and bans. Undeterred and unwavering, we continued the battle for the Reich's capital, without allowing

---

[61] Lichterfelde, Steglitz, and Wilmersdorf are localities in southwestern Berlin. Wittenbergplatz is located in central Berlin.

ourselves to be perturbed in the slightest by fear or anxiety of a looming ban.

The SA had passed its first major test. Much earlier than the Party itself, the SA had to overcome the crisis and start the fight. In just a few weeks, the limits imposed on the formerly small sect had shattered, and the movement had a name and rank. Our wounded certainly filled the hospitals, and the most seriously injured were left bedridden in our own infirmary. Some were struggling to stay alive.

SA men were arrested without cause and thrown into prison by the dozens. After a long, grueling investigation, there would be a trial in which the SA man, who had merely defended himself, stood accused, while the cowardly communist agitator was both witness and prosecutor. Neither the police nor the government provided us with the protection to which we were constitutionally entitled. What else could we have done, other than try to help ourselves? We were not yet a mass Party with imposing numbers. The movement was a small lost group that set out with fierce desperation to root out the Jewish demon within the capital of the Reich.

Scorned, mocked, reviled, spat upon, slandered by cowardly vitriol, degraded as pariahs, and branded as dead men walking, yet the SA men of Berlin persisted, marching behind the blazing red swastika flag, confident of a better future.

It is impossible to name everyone who made lasting contributions to the progress of the movement in Berlin. Those who sacrificed their blood and lives for the movement will not be individually recorded in the Party's history book. But the SA as a whole, as a political combat formation, its activist will, its courageous and firm action, its quiet and sober heroism, its disciplined behavior—all this will be unforgettable in the history of the National Socialist movement.

*   *   *

This proud attitude is not borne by any one individual. It is the organization as a whole, the SA as a troop, the brown army as a movement. But above all this, the unknown SA man, with his fighting spirit, raises his eternal face, quiet, admonishing, and demanding. It is this political soldier, who stood up in the National Socialist movement, doing his duty in the service of an ideal, in silence and indifferent to glory, obeying a law that he sometimes does not even know, that he only understands by listening to his heart. In his presence, we are filled with awe.

Spandau SA standard-bearer

5. Bloody Ascent

Before the emergence of Marxism, terror as a tool of political struggle was completely unknown. It was the Social Democrats who would use it to impose their political ideas. The SPD is the leading political party supporting the ideology of Marxist class struggle. It claims to be pacifist, but that does not prevent it from sowing the seeds of the bloodiest of civil wars throughout the country. When the SPD made its first political appearance, the bourgeois state stood firmly opposed. The parliamentary parties had already fossilized and hardened, and it seemed impossible to reach the masses through democratic or parliamentary channels.

If the bourgeoisie had recognized and fought the Marxist danger from the start, not only its symptoms but also its root cause, then it would have been impossible for Marxism to win any appreciable support in Germany. The German worker, by his nature and disposition, has neither an internationalist nor pacifist spirit. He is indeed a son of the German people, who are nationalistic and ready to fight. Because Marxism taught him that the dictatorship of the proletariat could only be achieved through pacifist internationalism, the German worker accepted this ideology that is so foreign to his existence. Contrary to what its name might suggest, the SPD, in its conception, was not at all democratic.[62] As long as it was the parliamentary minority, it pursued the exact same goals as modern communism with the exact

---

[62] SPD stands for *Sozialdemokratische Partei Deutschlands* (Social Democratic Party of Germany).

same methods; only after the capitalist mutiny of November 1918, when the Social Democrats firmly held power in their hands and could establish themselves through parliamentary processes, did it suddenly become democratic.

Its past, however, proves precisely the opposite. It was a matter of blood and civil war, of terror and class struggle. They wanted to destroy the capitalist parties; they never tired of defiling the ideals of the nation and flouting the illustrious history of the German people with presumptuous impudence. The Social Democrats ruthlessly warred against the bourgeois state with the sole aim of building the dictatorship of the proletariat on its rubble.

In this struggle, partisan terrorism was of crucial importance. It was used so remorselessly that the bourgeois parties did not have the slightest chance of defending themselves against it on their own.

They had no choice but to resist the threat of this anarchy, with the help of the state, the police, and the army, and they thus provided the Social Democrats, even before the war, with the perfect opportunity for slander, for vile shameful provocation. The Imperial Guard, the spiked helmet, the brutal and narrow-minded policeman, the army that suppressed an intellectual movement in the service of capitalism—it was along these lines that the shameless and incessant insults of the Marxist press were spread, which the German Empire tolerated without complaint.

It was the fault of the bourgeoisie if Marxism was able to corrode and undermine the foundations of the state in this manner without preventing such subversive conduct. The state authority assumed that Marxism had to be tolerated and that, in a state of emergency, the Social Democrats would not ignore the needs of the nation. The political bourgeoisie was systematically kept under this illusion.

Finally, in the hour of need, the last representative of the German Empire appealed to the syndicate of professional traitors with these words: "I no longer know any parties, only Germans!"[63] Thus opening, in the midst of war, the door to Marxist anarchy. In those grim days after Scheidemann was appointed permanent secretary,[64] the

---

[63] These famous words were uttered on August 4th, 1914, by Wilhelm II, the last emperor to reign in Germany, in an attempt to mobilize the Germans for the First World War.

[64] Philipp Scheidemann was a member of the SPD. He was the permanent secretary for the German Empire during the First World War. As such, he was the chief government official who worked within the German government to undermine the German government. He pushed Wilhelm II to abdicate, and once he succeeded, he

history of monarchical Germany was already drawing to a close. Sixty years of vile, irresponsible partisan agitation succeeded in bringing about the collapse of the old Germany. The Social Democrats quit the warpath and moved into office.

From this point on, moderate Marxism changed tactics. The blood-soaked revolutionaries who had organized the revolution under the Phrygian cap were suddenly transformed into well-off, capitalist fat cats, once the old Reich fell.[65] Those who previously sang "The Internationale" now elevated the "Deutschlandlied" to the national anthem.[66] They quickly learned to navigate the diplomatic arena of parliament adroitly, but they did not intend to abandon their original goals.

The SPD will forever remain what it has always been. At best, it will agree to temporarily modify its political tactics and the methods it uses in the daily struggle. As long as it is in power, it will swear by peace and order, and will encourage the limited intelligence of its followers to respect the authority of the state. But as soon as it is removed from power, it will return to the opposition, and the methods it uses to fight the government then will be exactly the same ones that it used before the war.

The conception of the state, behind which the SPD hides deceitfully and hypocritically today, is only a pretext for it. The state for Social Democrats is first and foremost their own party. They identify their selfishly partisan interests with the interest of the state, and when a *Zahlabend* strategist speaks about "protecting the Republic," he only thinks of his coterie whom he wants to protect from public criticism via state censorship.[67] Marxism has never changed, and it never will. We see what its essence is when a new political movement

---

"proclaimed" the new Weimar Republic, ending his speech with the words, "The old and rotten, the monarchy, has collapsed. Long live the new! Long live the German Republic!"

65 The Phrygian cap, also known as the cap of liberty, was a piece of headwear given to Roman slaves on their emancipation. It eventually grew into a symbol of republicanism, egalitarianism, and liberty more generally.

66"The Internationale" is a revolutionary song, originally composed in France in the late nineteenth century, and later adopted as the anthem of various far-left, radical movements; a translated version of it would eventually become the national anthem of the Soviet Union. The "Deutschlandlied" has been the German national anthem since 1922, when it was selected by the first Weimar president.

67 The *Zahlabend* was a monthly meeting in various socialist organizations. They would be required to pay monthly dues at these meetings and would engage in discussion about the political and social life as seen through the socialist worldview.

stands up to it and challenges it. Then the SPD suddenly returns to its methods of the past, and the same combat methods that it purportedly rejects and denounces as contemptible seem good enough to it now to use ruthlessly against the new adversary.

Terrorism grew with the SPD, and as long as there is a Marxist organization in Germany, it will never disappear from the political arena. But if Marxism ruthlessly uses partisan terror tactics, then its political adversary must under no circumstances renounce brute force, for his own protection, because he would thus be entirely at the mercy of Marxist terrorism. In the long run, this becomes all the more unbearable, because Marxism has been firmly established in public offices since 1918, and thus acts as a far more dangerous counterpart to partisan terror. As a result, not only will the gangs of communist thugs on the street crush every nationalist tendency and all those who express an opposing opinion, but moreover, the authorities and the civil administration will assist them. The consequence is that the German mentality is left defenseless against the terror tactics of the streets and the government.

How many times our SA men, who had only exercised the most basic right of self-defense, were brought before the courts and punished with long prison sentences and hard labor as miscreants! It is understandable that under such conditions the anger of the nationalist opposition has reached a boiling point. The means of defending oneself against terror tactics have been taken away from the nationalist elements of Germany. The police refuse them the protection of life and limb to which every citizen is entitled. If, after all this, a peace-loving man defends his life with bare fists in an act of ultimate desperation, then he is dragged before the courts.

It is clear to any reasonable man that the Marxist press has no right whatsoever to punish National Socialism under the guise of public order. Marxism attacks any nonconformist opinion with terror, and when such an opinion defends itself, the journalist scum, using its all-too-familiar tactics, shout "Stop the thief!" to clue in the authorities. They seek to make the people believe that National Socialism threatens public order and safety, that it sows hatred and discord between classes and professions, that this is the reason why it has no political value and must be judged in court.

The nationally conscious government of the future will have the privilege of once again proclaiming the most basic right of self-defense for a Germany of Germans. Today, we have reached the point where anyone who still dares to embody Germanness is inherently stigmatized and designated as the political target. From this fact alone, the Marxist creature concludes he has the right—in fact, the duty—to assault the nationally conscious German, even with weapons.

A march through communist Neukölln

The Hitler Youth is marching!

The SA is marching!

The intentions of Marxism in using this tactic are clear. Marxists know that their power rests essentially on controlling the streets. As long as only they could claim leadership of the masses and intervene in political decisions with pressure from the streets, they had no reason to use violence against the bourgeois parties that tolerated them in silence. But when the National Socialist movement emerged and demanded the same rights that Marxism considered its exclusive domain, the SPD and the KPD were forced to confront it with terrorism. Facing a nationalist worldview based on logic, their intellectual arguments failed them, and thus the dagger, the revolver, and the baton had to decisively make up for this.

The bourgeois parties still persist in the error of believing that there is a fundamental difference between social democracy and communism. They want to de-radicalize social democracy so it can participate in the political responsibility of the state. This is both senseless and futile, because social democracy will only assume this responsibility as long as it controls the state. As soon as it loses its ability to influence politics, it will flout authority, attempt to disturb public peace and safety with terror tactics, and will not rest until it has toppled the enemy government.

The cowardice of the bourgeois parties in the face of Marxism is utterly unprecedented. They are incapable of mobilizing the people. The bourgeois will be ready, when the time comes, to vote for his party, but nothing can persuade him to take to the streets to defend the political goals his party pursues.

It is quite different with National Socialism. At the beginning, it could not fight in the legislature. Very early on, it used modern means of activism: leaflets, posters, public meetings, street demonstrations. In doing so, it very quickly came up against Marxism, and the fight naturally became inevitable. Ultimately, we had to employ the same methods used by Marxism if we wanted to bring our struggle to a successful conclusion.

The National Socialist movement had no reason to unleash partisan terror tactics on its own initiative. Its aim was to conquer the masses, and it felt so sure of its own rights that it could renounce all violence with a clear conscience. It only resorted to violence when violence was used against it.

A treacherous corner

And this quickly became the case—especially in those years when the National Socialist movement was still weak, when the adversary could hope to drown it in its own blood, when its supporters were being killed in the streets, believing that he was breaking the movement up and forcing it to disband from the outside. Marxism intended to bring National Socialism to its knees using the same methods it had employed before with such great success against the bourgeois parties.

A march through Spandau

However, Marxism was very wrong about that. National Socialism recognized Marxism for what it was from the very beginning. It
had understood that Marxists would resort to their favorite method,
brute force, against whatever threatened them first. This is why the
National Socialist movement had to resolve to use the same methods
in the end.

While the path of the National Socialist movement is marked with
traces of blood, the bloodshed is not the fault of the Party alone.
Rather, it lies with those Marxist organizations that elevated terrorism
to the level of a political principle and acted on this principle for decades.

Marxism considers it a shameless act of arrogance when a non-
Marxist party appeals to the masses at all or when it dares to organize
public meetings and takes to the streets. The masses, the people, the
streets—these are, as Marxism would have us believe, the indisputa-
ble domains of social democracy and communism. Other parties can
attempt to play with parliament and trade associations, but only
Marxism has a right to the people.

Now, National Socialism is aimed precisely at this people. It appeals to the man on the street, it speaks his language, talks to him
about the trials and tribulations that oppress him, takes up the cause
of the people as its own. And this instantly creates a menacing threat
to Marxism. In doing so, National Socialism has touched the weak
point of social democracy and communism, and attacked them from
a position where they can be defeated. The Social Democrats have
learned that they cannot suppress an intellectual movement in the

long term with mechanical tactics. On the contrary, violence always begets violence, and the more intense the pressure becomes, the greater the resistance.

It is not a sign of wisdom, let alone revolutionary attitude, on the part of the Social Democrats to continually attempt to counter National Socialism with official repression. The fact that they want to stigmatize National Socialists as lawbreakers points clearly to their insincere hypocrisy. This attempt would have always and everywhere failed miserably if the bourgeois press had echoed the truth and refused to provide support for the guilty, criminal actions of Marxism.

It is true that the bourgeois press completely corresponds to the character, or rather the lack of character, of the special interest groups in parliament representing it. They want peace for the sake of peace. They even bowed to the demands of Marxist terrorists, without daring to murmur a complaint. For better or worse, we have grown accustomed to it.

The bourgeois parties want to coexist with Marxism, without taking into account that Marxism will only respect the political truce with the bourgeoisie if they agree with Marxism in everything and if they give it free rein.

The National Socialist movement rejects this lazy compromise. It openly declared war on Marxism. Very quickly the ground on which this war was waged was littered with victims, and it is important to note here that bourgeois public opinion everywhere lacked the moral courage necessary to put itself with total commitment on the side of the right wing, which would, in the event of success, benefit them in the end.

Public opinion falls silent when National Socialist SA men are gunned down in the streets. In the bourgeois newspapers, such events are dismissed without the slightest comment in only a few lines at the bottom of the last page. As if there is no other way. The Marxist newspapers most often do not even mention it in passing. They systematically ignore everything that might incriminate their own organizations. If they are forced to provide explanations on specific points, they distort the facts, make the attacker the victim and the victim the attacker, cause a commotion, appeal to the public authorities, mobilize public opinion against National Socialism, and fulminate against a partisan terror that they themselves orchestrated and introduced into politics. And if by chance we so much as touch a hair on the head of a Marxist assassin in self-defense, the entire press shrieks with anger and indignation. National Socialists are portrayed as common bloodthirsty agitators, murderers of workers. We are even accused of bludgeoning and shooting harmless passers-by out of sheer pleasure in spilling blood.

For such outrageous behavior, the bourgeois newspapers have nothing left but "elegant silence." On the other hand, they have plenty to say when a Marxist thug is harmed after his victims defend themselves. But absolutely never is there any positive mention of National Socialists.

The Hitler Youth march through the communist southeast.

This has particularly devastating effects on the proletarian masses. Because National Socialists are relegated to second-class status, because they are considered the scum and dregs of humanity, the opinion has spread among the people that Marxists no longer need be judged according to the law. An injustice, considered outrageous and vexatious elsewhere, becomes quite natural here. A communist thug, whose usual line of work is political murder, is bound to his nature, always tempted to yield to his brutal instincts. He knows it in advance: the press will be silent, and public opinion will agree with him. Is he summoned to court? If so, then it is only as a witness—and at worst, if it goes wrong, he will get a few months in prison for possession of an unlawful weapon, which will then be pardoned or commuted owing to extenuating circumstances.

By hearing so much about the "political children" of social democracy, people have become accustomed to not taking communists seriously. People only see their violent tendencies as occasional gaffes and thus have a generous understanding and tolerance for them. They close their eyes when the communist press pushes for civil war, and they keep a compassionate heart for the Cheka mercenaries who murder a National Socialist under the cover of darkness like cowards.[68] They treat the victim with the same "loving kindness" that tabloids would treat a rapist or a serial killer.

The SA man suffers the consequences of these irresponsible actions. In the midst of the disgraceful calls for murder hurled toward him with impunity, he becomes nothing more than a man to be killed. He can be ridiculed and slandered, spit upon and terrorized, beaten and murdered. No one could care less. His own party cannot guarantee him protection. The state authorities refuse him; the press takes sides, not for him, but against him, and the public considers it entirely justified to chase him off the streets. If National Socialism were responsible for even a hundredth of the murders of which communism is guilty, the authorities would have long since eradicated it root and branch.

But communism is allowed to persist. We look at it with one eye laughing and the other crying. Basically, it is only fighting against National Socialism, a movement that is hated by all and enemy to all, against a party considered irritating and inconvenient competition everywhere it goes. This movement, however, cannot be fought with official methods alone and must be, according to those in power, fought in the streets.

This appalling irresponsibility was to have terribly serious repercussions, especially in Berlin. This city of four million inhabitants offers the safest asylum to seedy political elements. Marxism has been firmly embedded there for decades. There, it has its intellectual and physical headquarters, from which it leaks poison throughout the country. There, it has the masses in the palm of its hand and controls the many different branches of the political press. There, the police are at its service. There, National Socialism is suppressed by any means necessary—and it truly is necessary for them, because if National Socialism conquers Berlin, then Marxist supremacy in Germany will meet its end.

---

[68] The Cheka was the secret police under the Soviet regime, charged with the persecution and suppression of political opposition. It murdered many perceived enemies of Vladimir Lenin's regime from its formation in 1917 until 1922, when it was replaced by a different organization. *Battle for Berlin* was first published in 1932, a decade after the Cheka was dissolved, so the term is being used figuratively here.

"Yes, we can!" One of Mjölnir's drawings.

*   *   *

People have more compassionless and harsh minds in Berlin than in any other city in the Reich. The breathtaking speed of this asphalt monster made its residents heartless and soulless. The hunt for happiness and the struggle for sustenance take on more cruel forms in Berlin than in the provinces. Communal ties have been totally severed here. The Reich's capital is populated by seething masses that have yet to be given inner discipline and a greater spiritual impetus.

Social misery also produces completely different outgrowths in this city than in the rest of the Reich. Year after year, thousands upon thousands of people from the provinces travel to Berlin, seeking satisfaction that is most often unattainable. With boundless ambition, they challenge fate in an effort to rise up, only to quickly sink back, discouraged and burned out, into the formless mass of the anonymous proletariat of the great metropolis.

In fact, the working class of Berlin is truly without a natural habitat. They already consider themselves lucky to only eke out their hopeless and joyless existence in some tenement block. Many are condemned to languish in unoccupied houses and under bridges in a life of despair without a home or any belongings, an existence more like hell.

Marxism found in this city a ready-made ground for its anarchic and destructive tendencies. Its ideology is disconnected from reality, yet it found willing listeners here. They eagerly received it and believed in it as if it were a divine promise of salvation that would drive out every need and misery. Marxism had firmly established its positions in Berlin. When National Socialism attacked, it defended itself by spreading the lie that the National Socialist movement intended to undermine and sow dissension among the international proletariat and its Marxist organizations, all for the benefit of the powers of capitalism. In this crucial struggle, the Social Democrats and communists were united; in the shadow of this lie, the proletariat saw National Socialism as nothing more than a ruthless troublemaker, a shameless enemy to the interests of the international working class.

It did not take long for Marxism to recognize the danger of the National Socialist movement. In other cities, it had merely mocked, reviled, or slandered the movement for years. In Berlin, after only two months of fighting, it caught a glimpse of the disaster that awaited it and immediately began to use the bloodthirsty terror tactics that it used in the rest of the Reich much too late, to its own detriment.

It is well known that persecution only ever defeats the weak, but the strong emerge from it, building strength from the adversity. Thus, any violence that is used ultimately hardens one's determination.

It was the same with us. The movement had to endure unimaginable Marxist terrorism. From time to time, we came very close to giving up. But in the end, indignation and inner passion always brought us back. We never gave in, in order not to offer our enemies the pleasure of witnessing our defeat under the mercilessness of their blows.

The strongest bonds are cemented by blood. Every SA man who fell, or who left the ranks of his comrades owing to severe injuries, passed onto them his resolution and indignation. What had happened to him could well happen another day to his comrade, and if he had been hit, it was the duty of his brothers in arms to ensure that the movement grew stronger and that none dared to hit him again. For each man assassinated, a hundred more men stood up. The blood-soaked flag did not bow. The firm hands of its bearers held it all the more defiantly.

We were not the ones who wanted this bloodshed; terror is neither a means to an end or an end in itself. With heavy hearts, we had to oppose violence with violence, in order to ensure the progress of the movement in people's minds. But we were in no way prepared to renounce the civil rights that Marxism wanted to arrogantly claim for itself alone.

We readily admit that our goal was to conquer the streets. Through the streets, we wanted to win over the masses and the people, and at the end of this path was political power. We had a duty to this, because, using political power, we wanted to defend not our own interests but those of the nation.

We did not breach the peace. Rather, it was breached by the Marxists, who refused to recognize the same rights for all and attempted to violently crush those who dared to even desire to share those rights that they claimed to have in their hands alone.

Perhaps the bourgeoisie will one day thank us for having re-established in Germany the right to freedom of opinion, at the cost of many violent deaths. Perhaps the bourgeois newspapers will recognize us for truly saving them from the intellectual slavery of Marxism and the oppressive terror of Bolshevism. We do not yearn for the sympathy of the bourgeoisie, but we believed we could at least count on the fair and objective recognition of their press in the struggle for the restoration of culture and true order of peace and discipline.

Our hopes were dashed. If today boundless contempt for bourgeois cowardice is found in many circles of the National Socialist movement, this is not the consequence of partisan agitation but rather a healthy and natural reaction to the lack of courage in their own convictions that the bourgeoisie have constantly demonstrated toward our movement. We are well aware of the excuses that certain sophists put forward in defense of this disgraceful attitude. They claimed that the way we led the struggle was not very refined, nor did it observe the good manners prevalent in educated circles. We are considered vulgar when we speak to the people in their own language, a language that some arrogant bourgeois will never speak, let alone understand.

That bourgeois wants peace for the sake of peace, even if he suffers under this rancid "peace." When Marxism conquered the streets, it retreated to safety like a coward. It hid behind the curtains, all intimidated and fearful, while the SPD chased the bourgeois worldview from public discourse and overthrew the edifice of monarchy in a massive attack. Bourgeois public opinion allies against National Socialism with the Jewish press. In doing so, the bourgeoisie dig their own grave and commit suicide, for fear of being killed by someone else.

In the interest of public peace . . .

However, what is most irritating is the hypocritical feature common between both the social democratic press and the communist press, which they try to keep secret in their fight against National Socialism. Sometimes *Die Rote Fahne* relies on the capitalist newspapers in its fight against our movement, which leaves us with only a pitying smile. Of course, the alliance is not so deep that they openly greet each other on Unter den Linden, [69] but when they are alone together, it is all still there. When we did pose a threat to their Jewish

---

[69] One of Berlin's busiest streets, Unter den Linden is a boulevard in the central district of Mitte. Goebbels is emphasizing the fact that the SPD and KPD like to publicly feign their opposition to one another, when in reality they coexist well.

interests, they did not hesitate for a moment to band together to defend the tribe.

Against us, they were always united. When it is important to drag one of our leaders before the courts, or to hide the murder of an SA man from the public, or to protect Marxist thugs with complicit lies, then this united front of despicable criminals always appears, ranging from the reddest communist rag spouting class struggle to the serious Jewish newspaper with an international audience. Then they strike in unison and make no secret of their alliance, shouting to the whole world that they were and are brothers of one blood and one mind.

I still vividly remember today an episode that took place during those bloody and dire months, after one of our public meetings in Berlin. The communist hordes surrounded the building where we had gathered, waiting for the moment when our SA men would come out so they could murder them. Several days earlier, the press had been riling them up and called for action against us. The authorities refused to protect us, and the bourgeois papers kept quiet about it.

Shortly before the end of the meeting, the police blocked the exits of the building. While they should, logically, have been concerned with dispersing the communist mercenaries lurking outside, they instead considered it their duty to only search the SA men leaving the meeting for weapons.

They found a few pocket knives, a few wrenches and maybe— my God!—a brass knuckle. Their owners were thrown into vans and Then a single SA man stepped in front of the officer in charge, took off his cap and asked in a modest tone without the slightest note of anger, "And where can we find our coffins, Captain?"

These few sarcastic words said it all. The National Socialist movement was disarmed and defenseless. It was abandoned by everyone, given over to public ostracizing, and when it found itself facing mortal danger with only a few modest means of self-defense, it was sent to court for breaching the peace.

Very rarely in history has an intellectual movement been countered as vilely and dirtily as ours. The supporters of a new worldview have rarely had to make such great material and human sacrifices to achieve their goals as we have. Never has the victorious march of an oppressed and persecuted party been as triumphant as that of our movement. It cost us blood, but this blood made us grow. It bonded us together. Our martyrs lived in the spirit of our battalions, and their

heroic example gave the survivors the strength and courage to persevere.

We have not capitulated to any opposition. Rather, we have overcome it using the same means they used against us. In this struggle,
our movement remained relentless, because fate itself had forged it
like the hardest steel. From its earliest years, it was exposed to persecution that no other party in Germany could have withstood.

Here for Hitler!

That it triumphed is unmistakable proof that it was not only called
but chosen. If fate had desired otherwise, the movement would have
drowned in blood early on, but fate clearly had greater plans for us.
Our mission was ordained in history, and that is why we were tested,
it is true, but the mission was fulfilled once the ordeal was over.

In the years that followed, the movement marched on from one
victory to another. Many a member who joined our ranks later could
barely understand this. They must have thought that we were too
lucky and feared that the movement would end up suffocating under
its own triumphs.

They then forgot, if they had ever known it, how hard the Party had fought for every advantageous position. Subsequent success was only the just reward for previous steadfastness: fate neither favored nor spoiled us. It only gave us, generously of course but only after a very long wait, what we had earned through years of tenacious courage and perseverance.

While Germany was sinking, while a preposterous political system was selling off the last vestiges of German wealth to international high finance in an attempt to pursue an unrealizable and insane policy, we have declared war on decadence in all areas of public life.[70] In Berlin, as well as throughout the rest of the Reich, this struggle was undertaken by a handful of fanatical, determined men. The manner in which they carried it out won them friends, supporters, and enthusiastic followers over time. From a hundred they became a thousand. From a thousand they became a hundred thousand. And now, amid the chaotic collapse of German order, stands an army of millions of ambitious and single-minded fighters.

In Berlin, too, we had to endure much of the suffering and persecution that had plagued the entire movement. The Berlin movement has proven itself to be quite a match for them. The first National Socialists in the Reich's capital mustered the courage to take such risks, and in those risks, they finally conquered fate. They surmounted the obstacles and triumphantly carried their flag to the helm of the freshly awoken capital city.

The path our party followed was marked with blood, but the seed we sowed bore fruit. We were walking over graves, but we marched forward!

---

[70] The "unrealizable and insane policy" that was being pursued was the *Erfüllungspolitik*, or "policy of fulfillment," as adopted by the Weimar system. It advocated for fully complying with the Treaty of Versailles, which was signed in 1919, ending the First World War. It left the German Reich militarily defenseless and in economic shambles. The entire German nation was in essence declared criminals, and many Germans considered it a disgraceful national humiliation. The inhumanly harsh reparations amounted to hundreds of billions of US dollars, at today's rates; this was at the time of the Great Depression which was already exceptionally severe in Germany.

6. Outlawed!

The police chief of Berlin holds executive power in Prussia, and as Berlin is the seat of the Reich's government, German politics in general and Prussian politics in particular are practically in the hands of the Berlin police chief. The Berlin police department, more than any other in the entire Reich, therefore has a decidedly political character, and the police chief's office is almost always occupied by a politician.

As long as the Social Democrats were the legislative minority, the police chief of Berlin was their favorite target of fury, vitriol, and mendacious demagoguery. It was naturally the police chief of Berlin who was responsible for maintaining order in the Reich's capital. This constantly resulted in new conflicts between the police force and revolutionary Social Democrats. We all know how the chief of police of the Prussian monarchy, Traugott von Jagow, tried to assert himself in the face of Marxist insolence with this popular remark, "The street is for traffic. Let those who are curious what will happen be warned."[71] That was at a time when the Social Democrats were not yet loyal to the state, but on the contrary were trying to undermine and wear down, by all methods of propaganda, what it considered to be the loathsome framework of the state. The German Empire no longer had any ideals to counter the growth of Marxism. That is why it lacked the brutality and uncompromising rigor necessary to repress

---

[71] Traugott von Jagow was the conservative chief of police in Berlin from 1906 to 1916; when a collective of Marxists wished to register their demonstration to occupy the streets, Jagow famously uttered those words to express his disapproval.

Marxism's destructive tendencies. The consequence of this criminal negligence reared its ugly head on November 9th, 1918, when the masses rebelled and seized executive power, installing revolutionary Social Democrats into the seats of power.[72]

From that moment on, the Social Democrats saw the post of Berlin police chief as one of its many reserved political domains. Since then, the strongman of Alexanderplatz has been, without exception, put in place by this party.[73] Despite all the corruption that subsequently flourished and spread in this administration, the parties aligned with the Social Democrats were not convinced, at least in the Reich's capital, to take this post away from the extremist organization. Men like Richter, Friedensburg, Grzesinski, and Zörgiebel followed in a muddled succession at Alexanderplatz, one after the other.[74]

By taking over the Berlin police department, the Social Democrats were in control. It was now easy for them to provide their own organization with the opportunity to develop in complete freedom and to suppress and overpower any opinion hostile to the administrative powers. The Social Democrats' police department had no qualms during the years 1918 to 1920 about protecting itself from the Bolshevik danger by using the Freikorps and other volunteer units.[75] But as soon as the Red Terror had been defeated in the streets, the Social Democrats hastened to move on to fight against the nationalist movement. The main task of this extermination campaign rested in the hands of the Berlin police chief.

Whoever holds the Berlin police headquarters holds Prussia, and whoever holds Prussia holds the Reich. This axiom, which was valid

---

[72] The Social Democrats were one of many parties involved in the revolt against the German Empire, which ultimately fell with the Kaiser's abdication on November 9th, 1918.

[73] The "strongman" in this case is the chief of police.

[74] Wilhelm Richter, Ferdinand Friedensburg, Albert Grzesinski, and Karl Zörgiebel all served as the chief of police of Berlin during the time of the Weimar system.

[75] The Freikorps were originally irregular formations of volunteer combatants. In the aftermath of the First World War, they would often find themselves fighting Marxist and anarchist revolutionaries in the German Revolution of 1918, in defense of the Weimar system. The Social Democrats initially supported that revolution—until they seized power for themselves, at which point they wanted the revolution to end. The Bolshevik elements, however, were not satisfied with so-called social democracy and continued their insurrection. Thus, the Social Democrats called upon the right-wing Freikorps to help suppress the Marxist rebels. Many Freikorps members would later align with the NSDAP against the Weimar system.

during the time of the German Empire, was adopted literally by the
Marxist political forces that seized power in 1918. The Social Democrats took over the police department of Berlin and from that moment on, defended it very fiercely. By seizing the most important
Prussian ministries, they established themselves in this *Land*, the largest *Land* in fact,[76] and thus gained a decisive influence on the affairs
of the Reich, even when those affairs were handled by a cabinet over
which it did not have direct control. A conflict would only be inevitable between the growing National Socialist movement in Berlin and
the Social Democratic police department. We really did not need to
provoke it; it was part of the nature of things, and in fact, it broke
out the moment the National Socialist movement emerged from anonymity.

Dr. Bernhard Weiss, deputy chief of police in Berlin.

At the time, the Social Democrat Zörgiebel reigned at Alexanderplatz. For a position so heavy with responsibility and so difficult
to fill, he had no other qualification than being a member of their
party. To carry out his duties, he did not hesitate to use any means
necessary and hardly bothered with scruples.

At his side was Dr. Bernhard Weiss, a Jew, serving as his deputy
chief. He had gradually worked his way up from an administrative
career, later joined the police, and at a young age became head of the

---

[76] Under the Weimar system, Germany was divided into seventeen *Länder* (singular
Land). A *Land* was a federal administrative division of Germany, and Prussia was by
far the largest of the German *Länder*.

main department at Alexanderplatz, which was the political police.[77] He became a close collaborator of Severing after his first appointment as Prussian Minister of the Interior.[78] After Friedensburg was removed from office, Dr. Weiss was then appointed deputy chief of police. It is impossible to say that this man was able to provide the necessary impartiality toward National Socialism so that he could carry out his high office objectively. Dr. Weiss was Jewish. He openly professed Judaism and was a leader in major Jewish organizations and associations. Of course, he complained to the courts when National Socialists called him a Jew. The fact remains that he was without a doubt a Jew, outwardly and inwardly. The National Socialist movement is anti-Semitic, but it upholds an anti-Semitic view that is very dissimilar to those of Stoecker and Kunze.[79] Our anti-Jewish attitude is entirely principled; we certainly do not hold the Jews solely responsible for all the misfortune that has befallen Germany since 1918. We see in the Jew only the typical representative of decadence. He is a parasitic life form that, above all, thrives on and exploits the muddy morass of dying cultures.

When the last barriers separating international Jewry from the government in Prussia fell, the fate of the nation was sealed. From that day on, the infiltration of spiritual rootlessness into the areas of administrative discipline and national solidarity began, and there was no stopping the catastrophic collapse of the German state.

---

[77] The Berlin police had multiple divisions. The two main divisions were the criminal police (Kriminalpolizei) and the so-called political police (Geheimpolizei). The criminal police were primarily responsible for criminal investigations, and its members were ordinary police officers and detectives. The "political police" (also known as Abteilung IA or Section 1A) was, in essence, the secret police of Prussia that investigated crimes of a political nature. During his career, Weiss served in both divisions in leadership roles. Weiss would eventually restructure the political police to make it more efficient, and was a fervent proponent of the secret police under the Weimar system—perhaps ironically, as he was eventually purged from the over-politicized police force in 1932 for his republican affiliations and his Jewish identity.

[78] Carl Severing was a Social Democrat who had served in multiple political posts. He was politically centrist for the most part.

[79] Adolf Stoecker was a Lutheran theologian and noted anti-Semite in nineteenth-century Germany. Richard Kunze was a political organizer also noted for his anti-Semitism. Both individuals founded their own political parties, with Kunze's being a rival party to the NSDAP for a short period.

Alexanderplatz in Berlin

The fact that Jews were able to occupy high-ranking government positions at all is a telltale symptom of Germany's sunken state and unscrupulous perversion of fundamental political convictions since 1918. No sooner had the National Socialist movement made its debut in Berlin than the police department took commensurate countermeasures. The cold indifference kept toward us until then suddenly became active interest. Suddenly, our meetings were swarming with informants from Alexanderplatz. Every parade, every demonstration, every staff meeting was kept under meticulous police surveillance. Official informants, dubbed eight-penny boys in Berlin slang,[80] were sent to join the organization, in hopes of gathering necessary evidence so that, in the event of a clash, the movement could be wiped out with an official ban.

We were convinced that the lifeblood of the entire operation was the deputy police chief, Dr. Bernhard Weiss himself. And just as the Social Democrats before the war fought not only a system set against them but also those who obviously represented it, so too did we have to adapt our tactics to include not only Alexanderplatz but the police chief himself in our political attacks, whether we wanted to or not.

---

[80] "Eight-penny" refers to the meager remuneration for which the informants would betray the movement.

This explains why our fight against the methods used against us by the police department, the painful effects of which we were to feel very soon, focused more and more on the person of Dr. Weiss, second in command to the police chief. We had found in him a target that we could not have imagined better.

The mask protects its owner from police brutality and looks very democratic.

Dr. Weiss brings many things with him to his post that do not belong to it and few things that do, at least according to a normal person's understanding. For example, he is neither a professional policeman nor an avowed politician. He does, however, belong to the Jewish race, and that immediately aroused suspicion in our eyes. God only knows how he came to be called Isidor. We later had to convince ourselves that this epithet had been given to him and that in reality he simply bore the more harmless name Bernhard. In any case, I have to admit that if the name Isidor were not his actual name, it was at least a good one. Once again, Berlin's popular wit proved to be intact and spot-on by giving this man a nickname that seemed to fit him like a glove.

In later years, we were often handed severe prison sentences and heavy fines for having given this man a name that he considered an insult, so much so that he had it prosecuted in the courts, even though it was not in itself an insult. Despite his best efforts, he became well known by this name. He went down in contemporary history, and our massive attacks on him eventually made him one of the most popular targets of the anti-Semitic struggle of National Socialism.

"Dr. Weiss!" It soon became a memorable catchphrase. Every National Socialist knew it, and every activist had his physiognomy stamped into his memory, vividly and clearly, thanks to thousands of satirical magazines, photographs, and caricatures. He was seen as the soul of the fight against our movement, insofar as this fight was being led by the police department. He was held responsible for all the wrong done to us by Alexanderplatz. Since Dr. Weiss, unlike many of the other important figures in the Weimar system, was extraordinarily sensitive, National Socialist campaigning focused on turning him into a comical figure, without taking him seriously as a political adversary, mainly to lampoon him in situations that were not very flattering for him but that tallied with the natural taste of the Berlin public who love wit, whimsy, and satire.

Not a week went by without us having to engage in some sort of quarrel with Dr. Weiss. He had become the main target of our unrelenting attacks. We brought him out of the shadowy yet all the more influential anonymity of existence on the margins and into the bright light of public attention. Our rigorous sarcastic campaigns dealt him such blows that friend and foe alike enjoyed it.

Needless to say, all this was very frowned upon by Alexanderplatz, especially since they could hardly retaliate as we scored by making everybody laugh. Instead of actually defending himself, Dr. Weiss retreated to the safety of his office and sought to replace with measures of authority what he clearly seemed to lack in intellectual means.

Immediately after the violent and fateful clash at the Lichterfelde-Ost train station, I was summoned by the police department and was told in a rather blunt manner that from that day on our movement was just asking to be banned and that this would happen at the first opportunity. The struggle between the NSDAP and the police department had thus reached its turning point and what followed was only inevitable.

On May 1st, 1927, for the first time, Adolf Hitler spoke at a large meeting in Berlin. At the time, he was still banned from giving speeches throughout the Reich, which is why we had to call this meeting private—that is to say, open only to members. It took place at Clou, an old concert hall in central Berlin. We had chosen this site to avoid, owing to the date, any attempt to provoke the communists.[81] Our intention was not to make this event a combative rally, but rather to give new impetus to the National Socialist Party with the first public appearance of the Führer in the Reich's capital. This event would also provide the public with proof of the progress we had made.

"Great photo! They're cheaper by the dozen!"

The meeting was a success beyond all expectations. Clou's spacious rooms were packed to the rafters with registered Party members, and Hitler's speech, in all its rigor and profundity, was like a

---

[81] May 1st is celebrated globally as International Workers' Day, also known as May Day. In theory, it is similar to the American holiday of Labor Day; however, it is strongly associated with communist and socialist parties. At the time the author is speaking of, Marxist political organizations and labor unions were encouraged by the Second International (an international communist organization) to "energetically" protest in the streets for the Marxist conception of labor rights.

thunderbolt for all the listeners, most of whom had never seen or heard him before.

The press in the capital could not pass over this event in silence. It had to express its opinion about it one way or another. And so it did, in its usual way. Even before the meeting had begun, a Jewish weekly published an account of it. The article was full of insults, innuendo, and disgraceful lies. It equated Hitler with hardened criminals and vilified the movement in a downright incendiary way.

The fact that the newspaper had been printed and sold before the start of the meeting, thus giving eloquent witness to the dishonesty of those Jewish hacks, particularly incensed the Berlin comrades and filled them with indignation.

The following day's articles in the Jewish press were no match for this journalistic indignity. The mood among the Party comrades was thus brought to a boil, especially when it was noticed that the so-called nationalist and non-socialist press not only failed to raise an objection to this journalistic corruption, but also snubbed Hitler's first appearance in Berlin with insulting silence or a few empty, derisive remarks.

Text in thought bubble: "I'm at the police department!" Figure behind desk: "Zörgiebel."

We had to take a stand; our self-respect demanded it. To accept this without protest would have constituted a moral failure on the part of the National Socialist movement. As we still lacked a journalistic firm of our own in Berlin, we organized a public meeting for May 4th at the Kriegervereinshaus. It was intended as a protest against the shady financial maneuvers that had just been engineered by the Darmstädter Bank and its owner Jakob Goldschmidt.[82] A few weeks earlier, we caused a stir when we had held a mass demonstration against this typical representative of international finance and brought him to the attention of the public for the first time. This second event was to be a continuation of the first, and I then decided, before dealing with that particular issue as a speaker, to respond in the strongest terms to the attacks in the press concerning Hitler's visit to Berlin.

In this regard, it is worth mentioning that after Hitler's speech a Jewish newspaper in Berlin published an interview with Hitler that in fact had never taken place. A journalist called me to request this supposed interview. I categorically refused it, and I had to discover to my boundless amazement that, despite being clearly fake and made up from beginning to end, it appeared the next day in the press. All the provincial newspapers under Jewish influence circulated the interview. It was full of nothing but malicious vulgarity and despicable turpitude. Hitler, who totally abstains from alcohol as is well-known, was portrayed as a disgraceful drunkard. The vilest part of this journalistic outrage was that the author of the article attempted to give the impression that he, the representative of a Jewish newspaper, had spent an entire evening drinking with Hitler and thus had the best opportunity to observe him up close.

The Kriegervereinshaus was full to capacity, causing police to refuse entry to late arrivals. I began my speech with a rigorous examination of the yellow press in the Reich's capital and did not fail to ruthlessly pillory the Jewish scoundrel with the help of unassailable

---

[82] At this time, Darmstädter Bank was officially known as Darmstädter und Nationalbank (often shortened to Danatbank), and it was Germany's third largest bank. Jakob Goldschmidt was one the most influential Jews in the sphere of economic policy. Not only did he quickly become the senior partner of the Danatbank, Goldschmidt himself held over one hundred supervisory board mandates in other banks in addition to his daily bank management activities. For his "services to the German economic recovery," an honorary doctorate of political science was bestowed upon him in 1927. How great his contribution to this recovery really was could be seen when the Danatbank was eventually brought to the brink of collapse by his poor financial policy in 1931; in fact, in the summer of that year, the German government issued a special emergency decree so that not too many people in Germany would fall into economic ruin, after the entire German people had been reduced to beggars only eight years earlier by the inflation caused and exploited by Jewry.

evidence. I read the press reports one by one to the crowd as it listened attentively to my words, and after each one I counterposed it to the truth. This had an astonishing effect, and the audience was soon filled with an ever-growing anger that found its expression in loud cries of indignation.

As I had just finished settling accounts with these journalists and was about to move on to the main topic, an individual, seemingly in a state of drunkenness, stood up in the middle of the room. Through the thick haze of tobacco smoke I saw a head, the same color as the wine he drank, poking up among the crowded people. I heard, to my great surprise, this impertinent agitator disrupt the orderly meeting with his arrogant and offensive heckling. At first I pretended not to notice. The audience, shocked by this brazen behavior, froze for a moment in breathless silence. In this deep silence, that creature repeated his grossly offensive shouting toward me so as to provoke the listeners. And that seemed all the more outrageous as I had given no pretext, to anyone and in any way, for such shameful conduct.

I understood immediately that we were obviously dealing with an agitator, so I determined to resolve the incident as quickly as possible without being provoked. I paused my speech for a few seconds and turning toward the troublemaker, said to him in a dismissive tone, "So you want to disrupt the meeting! Would you like us to exercise our rights and invite you outside for some fresh air?" When the individual did not want to sit himself down again but instead tried to continue his provocations, a few courageous SA men came up, gave him a couple of slaps, grabbed him by the nape of the neck, and threw him out of the room.

All this only lasted a few seconds. The audience itself remained calm during it all. They only punctuated this attempt at completely senseless disruption with a few loud remarks of their own and cheered when the troublemaker had been removed and the speech could continue without incident.

Personally, I had not attached any significance to such an event. From the rostrum, I could only see that the agitator left the room with some rough handling. I then calmly continued my speech, discussing the actual topic of the meeting. The speech lasted an hour and a half, and as no one debated me, the meeting ended there. The audience was about to cheerfully leave the room when the police entered, naturally greeted by jeers and whistling from the peaceful crowd. A police officer climbed onto a chair and addressed the jumbled crowd in a raised voice. It was impossible to understand a single word. I myself had to call for silence, which soon came. The policeman was then able to inform the crowd he had orders to search every visitor for weapons. I stated that we would comply in silence and without protest with this measure, and the meeting became perfectly calm and quiet again. During the two hours it took to search the two to three thousand people, there were no clashes or any friction.

Poster for the meeting on May 4th, 1927.

The whole affair was over, or at least so I thought, but there was one thing I failed to consider. The next morning, I learned with surprise while reading the press that something extraordinary had happened at our assembly. The agitator we expelled was indeed a drunkard and a wretch, but he was also an actual pastor, although he clearly did not prove himself worthy of this title. But for the scavengers in the press, it was the fodder they had long sought. The same scoundrel journalists, who for decades had smeared with the slime of their cowardly slander anyone and everyone that wore a priest's vestments, now suddenly appointed themselves as the guardians of Christian morals and common decency. The drunkard was transformed into an elderly Reverend Father. His obscene, uncalled-for outburst became a harmless, modest interjection. The two Party members, who had taken the man outside, albeit not very gently, were reduced to homicidal Nazis. The couple of slaps to the face that this washed-up pastor had received turned into a brutal beatdown that shattered the skull of the poor victim, now fighting heroically against death in the hospital.

Close-up: Poster for the meeting on May 4th, 1927.

That was the signal. The press pounced on this harmless incident with sheer delight. It was blown up in accordance with all the customs of so-called journalistic integrity:

"They've crossed a line!"

"No more!"

"Enough of this criminal terror!"

"Must a pastor be beaten to death before the authorities do something about this?"

The Jewish media in the city went wild. This barrage from the press had clearly been prepared long in advance, inspired and nurtured by the authorities. On the night after the assembly, a meeting had taken place between the Berlin police department and the Prussian Ministry of the Interior.[83] The very next afternoon, a newspaper owned by Ullstein[84] announced the immediate ban of the NSDAP.[85] As always, the nationalist, non-socialist newspapers bowed to the Jewish mass hysteria like cowards without putting up any opposition. They did not even take the time to verify the facts. They took the same line, declaring with Pharisaic self-righteousness that when the political struggle takes such forms the authorities cannot be blamed for intervening with the full force of the law.

A united front, ranging from bourgeois patriotism to proletarian communism, had thus been formed. They were all calling for a ban on the already detested and irksome competitor. It was easy for the police department, thanks to this fabricated press campaign, to announce a ban and actually enforce it. We lacked the press to inform the public of what had really happened. We had no newspapers. A leaflet written the following day was confiscated by the police. After the bourgeois press had refused to serve the cause of justice, the movement's fate was decided.

Only one Berlin newspaper kept its nerve, defending our movement bravely and selflessly from the lies and slander of the Jewish journalists: the *Deutsche Zeitung*.[86] How this upright paper treated us

---

[83] The Ministry of the Interior had a mission roughly comparable to that of the US Department of Homeland Security or the British Home Office.

[84] Leopold Ullstein was the Jewish founder and publisher of several German newspapers, including at least one in Berlin.

[85] On May 5th, 1927, the NSDAP was banned by the police from activities in Berlin's metropolitan area. As a reminder, this is not the same ban that was instituted after the Beer Hall Putsch by the Bavarian government in November 1923.

[86] The *Deutsche Zeitung* was one of Berlin's smallest political daily newspapers. It was in print from 1896 to 1934 and had a very conservative and almost *völkisch* alignment.

will not be forgotten. Later, when we had become a great party of the masses, we had many friends in bourgeois-nationalist newsrooms. We never attached much value to these friendships; we knew what they were worth and remembered all too well the days when we were small and obscure, when the bourgeois scavengers took the petty pleasure of beating us senseless because everyone else was attacking us. The *Deutsche Zeitung*, on the other hand, let truth and justice speak for itself, thus proving that when the nationalist cause is at stake it had enough courage to brave unpopularity despite what public opinion might say.

*   *   *

The inevitable happened. Blow after blow. By noon the Jewish newspapers had already reported that a ban was unavoidable. We managed at the last moment to save the Party's postal checking account,[87] the most important files were secured, then we waited to see what would happen. Around seven o'clock in the evening, a messenger from the police department came to our office to deliver a registered letter. It was not difficult to guess that the ban on the Party was contained in this envelope, and I simply refused to accept the envelope from him. The courier retreated without having fulfilled his mission, but he pinned the letter on the door of the Party office. Since all was now lost anyway, we at least tried to save face for propaganda purposes. The letter was given to an SA man. He put on his full uniform one last time, left for the police headquarters, and actually managed to get to the police chief's office.

Once there he barged through the door, threw the letter into the room and shouted, "We National Socialists refuse to recognize the ban!" The next day, the press took this as an opportunity to comment on our obstinate temper and shameless contempt for the law. In the early hours of the morning, a large contingent of police officers arrived at our office and occupied the premises from the basement to the attic; every closet, desk, and shelf was sealed shut, and the ban was actually put into effect.

The National Socialist movement in Berlin had legally ceased to exist. It was a blow from which recovery would be difficult. We had

---

[87] Not as common in North America, postal savings systems are banking systems operated by and involving the national postal service.

succeeded in emerging from anonymity and prevailed against street terrorism; we had carried forward our ideal and its flag, unconcerned about the dangers that lay ahead. We had spared no pain and no effort to demonstrate to the people of the Reich's capital our goodwill and the sincerity of our intentions. To some extent, we had already succeeded. However, as the movement set out to break its last shackles and join the ranks of the major mass organizations, it was plunged into oblivion by a crushing ban. Little did we know then that this ban would by no means destroy the movement but would, on the contrary, give it new, unexpected strength. In fact, if it could survive this ordeal, it would be equal to any challenge.

That night I had a brief meeting with Hitler, who happened to be staying in Berlin. He immediately assessed the chain of events that had led to the ban, and we agreed that the movement had to prove it could master this difficult test. We sought to save what could be saved. Insofar as it was possible and feasible, we used the respectable press. Unfortunately, we could only modestly counteract the public defamation of the movement by the Jewish press. We did not achieve much, but we did manage to at least temporarily keep the nucleus of the Party intact.

Here too, of course, there was no shortage of know-it-alls, full of insight, who would suddenly emerge from their obscure anonymity to provide us the benefit of their sage advice now that the movement was banned, yet when we were fighting, they were nowhere to be found. The moment the signal to break off the battle was given, they would suddenly appear on the scene, not to cover the retreat but to further dishearten our troops with cowardly caviling.

I above all was the object of unscrupulous public slander. These bourgeois wretches claimed that the movement could very well have been preserved if only it had adopted a less radical and more restrained tone. All of a sudden, they had foreseen and foretold everything. That did not mean they were helping to piece together a new structure from the shattered remains of the collapsed organization; on the contrary, they were striving to foment wider discord and make the confusion worse.

The press was already reporting that my arrest was imminent. This was a barefaced lie, as I had not broken the law in any way. Nothing more than wishful thinking. The main purpose was to stir up public opinion against us.

At the time, the Jewish press first fabricated a rumor about an internal rift between Hitler and me, as a result of which I gave up my post as Berlin *Gauleiter* to take up the same position in Upper Silesia.[88] The rumor underwent the most colorful variations over the following years and has not stopped to this day. Every time the movement is about to strike hard or undergoes a temporary crisis, it reappears in the columns of Jewish newspapers, providing us with a renewed opportunity for cheer and joy. Here too, desire is taken for reality. They wanted us to believe that I had left Berlin, because I had obviously become an inconvenient nuisance. They hoped, after my departure, to find an opportunity to break up the Party from within.

The idea of such a departure did not even occur to me. Certainly I had thought, in the first few weeks of my work in Berlin, that this task would only be temporary and that, as soon as the resistance standing in the way of the movement in the capital of the Reich was overcome, I could cede my position to someone else, someone better. If I have persisted until today in this difficult and duty-laden position, it is due not only to the growing satisfaction that this work gives me but also—and indeed for a considerable part—to the fact that the Jewish press would prefer to see me gone. I never do what the Jews would want. They should beg me to stay in Berlin, and maybe then I would leave this city. As long as they want me to leave, I will stay, especially since I still have a few projects in mind and I intend to achieve other successes here.

It was only as the clash for the Reich's capital developed that the full scale of the task became clear to me. If we succeeded in conquering Berlin for National Socialism, our victory would be virtually complete. The capital of the Reich is indeed the center of the country; from here, currents of thought flow inexorably into the people. To win Berlin back to Germanness is a truly historic mission, well worth the efforts of the best among us.

In the midst of the storm unleashed against us by the press, I had to keep an old promise and leave for Stuttgart for two days.[89] And in the editorial columns, this was once again the occasion for boundless, inflammatory slander. It was declared that I had shirked my duties like a coward; it was rumored that I had fled in the face of imminent

---

[88] A *Gauleiter* was a political official who governed a *Gau* under the NSDAP's organization of Germany.

[89] Stuttgart is an industrial city on the Neckar River in western Germany and is the capital of Baden-Württemberg.

arrest. My absence from Berlin was used to mobilize public opinion against the Party and myself in the vague hope of driving a wedge between the Führer and his troops and shatter the tottering movement from within.

Once in Stuttgart, I learned that an irresponsible news agency in Berlin had spread the rumor that a warrant had been issued for my arrest. Disregarding this, I set off that same evening on my return journey, and despite a few loyal comrades who had come to meet me

An example of the press in Berlin reporting on the NSDAP's ban:
"The National Socialists are banned yet again."

as far as Halle to prevent me from returning to Berlin, I continued on my station, I was honored with a reception I would not have dared hope for, even in my wildest dreams.

The entire station platform was packed full with people. The entrance hall to the station was filled to capacity, and outside there was a crowd of fired-up Party members and supporters. Hundreds and thousands of people ran, without regard for the *Bannmeile*,[90] along Königgrätz Street and Potsdam Street behind my moving car, which could only barely make its way through the hustle and bustle. At night on this fine May evening resounded for the first time the battle cry, which was to become the inspiring slogan of the underground movement in Berlin for an entire year:

"Banned but not dead!"

Yes, the movement could not be killed. Not with terror and not with bans. It was beaten with a baton wherever it dared appear. It was without rights and without defense. The authorities put the screws to it, and the bloodthirsty Cheka pursued it, armed with daggers and revolvers. Despite repression and imprisonment, the proud eagles of our flags soared into the air. Our ideal was firmly anchored in the hearts of faithful supporters, and the flag fluttered gloriously at the head of the marching battalions. Bans and persecution were ultimately to provide the movement with the unbreakable resilience it needed to carry on the difficult battle that would decide the fate of the German people.

A new stage in our work now began. The organization was dislocated, and the legal framework of the Party dissolved. At first, it was impossible to rally the Party members around a new, solid center, because of course we did not cease operations under the ban. Added to this were hardships and abuse of all kinds, which only made our lives more difficult. The Party was monitored, kept under surveillance, and spied on in every possible way. The eight-penny boys followed us at every step, and even the slightest provocation was used against the movement.

The ban had been imposed by the police department, not under the Act for the Protection of the Republic, but under the ordinary civil law.[91] The purported excuse, which we received a few days later,

---

[90] The *Bannmeile* is a restricted area surrounding certain government buildings in which no public assemblies may be held.

[91] The Act for the Protection of the Republic was a law in the Weimar Republic designed to ban organizations that were deemed a threat to the constitutional order.

simply defied description. Since we could not defend ourselves, we did not bother with Alexanderplatz. It was assumed that the alleged crimes had been proven, yet no verdict had ever been reached. There was no mention at all of the meeting at the Kriegervereinshaus, but rather reference was made to things that had happened in the distant past. Since the harsh measures taken by the police department against us in enforcing the ban outraged Party members to an extreme, street demonstrations inevitably followed night after night, which were then used as a pretext to justify the ban.

They were wise to refrain from taking me to court as the press so impetuously demanded during their smear campaigns. There was nothing they could accuse me of. The entire press campaign was a blatant farce, staged with such brazen audacity only because we could not defend ourselves and public opinion simply refused our decent beliefs any protection.

Barely a few days later, anyone with any sense of objectivity and impartiality could see we were in the right. The retired Reverend Father, an old man named Fritz Stucke, his head picturesquely decorated with a white bandage, appeared at a meeting of the

Reichsbanner to tell the gangs of Social Democratic thugs about his heroic adventures in the war against National Socialism.[92]

A pastor as a member of the Reichsbanner! It was the end of a cowardly, shameful, and slanderous press campaign. The ecclesiastical authorities publicly declared that "the former pastor Stucke of the Nazareth Church had been dismissed from all functions within the church, for unbecoming conduct, by virtue of a final and absolute disciplinary ruling from the Evangelical Consistory of the March of Brandenburg" and that "he had thus lost the right to the title of pastor and the vestments of clergy within the Evangelical Church following the decision of the Court of Appeal on July 21st, 1923."

Our wings are growing back . . .

Furthermore, it was learned that this individual, despite his expulsion from the church, had a flourishing business giving eulogies and that his normal state was total drunkenness. His attempt at provocation in our meeting left only one question: was this the action of a drunkard or a paid mole? The answer, however, was useless, once the Party was banned and the press campaign abated. The Jewish press had achieved its goal, the barrage had forced public opinion to capitulate, a troublesome political adversary had been cleared away with

---

92 The Reichsbanner Schwarz-Rot-Gold, commonly known as the Reichsbanner, was an anti-fascist paramilitary formation under the Weimar regime. It would often engage in brawls against the SA and was eventually banned by the Third Reich.

the support of the state authority, and public conscience had been salved thanks to a manufactured mass hysteria.

A few days later, the KPD organized a large demonstration in the Sportpalast, during which a policeman dared enter the meeting hall.[93] There was not the slightest trace of provocation in this gesture, but it did not prevent him from being hit on the head with a mug of beer thrown at him from the stands. His skull was fractured, and he was admitted to the hospital in critical condition.

Our crime, how minor and tame in comparison! Despite that, not a hair on the head of the KPD was touched, as the communists are really the political offspring of the Social Democrats. They leave them alone because they may need them every now and then, and after all the KPD is their own flesh and blood.

A silent appeal: "Germany, awaken!"

National Socialism, on the other hand, was banned, even though it had often enough demonstrated its peaceful nature and had only responded to the most shameless attempts at provocation with un-faltering calm and iron discipline, because National Socialism is the absolute opponent of Marxism of all stripes. There can be no recon-ciliation between it and Marxism, but only a struggle to the point of annihilation. Linden Street knew it, Alexanderplatz knew it, and

---

[93] The Berlin Sportpalast was a large indoor arena in central Berlin with a public capacity of up to fourteen thousand individuals.

Bülowplatz knew it.[94] Thus they waited to strike at the right moment. Thus the hack journalists contaminated public opinion with the miasma of vile, false slander. Thus the authority of the state was appealed to, and articles of law, despised and scorned in other times, were utilized.

It was therefore not surprising that the Social Democrats would stand up for themselves, because they are, in the end, only fighting to save their own existence. But that the non-socialist parties and their scavenging journalists stooped to sell their services to Marxism, thus helping to bring down a movement that could not defend itself, will forever remain the deep shame of the bourgeois press and the parties that supported it.

They did not achieve their goal. The day after the ban, Prussia's highest dignitaries went to great lengths to demonstrate in one of Ullstein's ultra-capitalist publications that there was no place in Berlin for National Socialism.

Once and for all! If we had not already known it from their activity elsewhere, the outrageous events that took place on Wednesday during the rally at the Kriegervereinshaus demonstrate once again that the so-called National Socialist Workers' Party is not a political movement, but rather a gang of rowdy and violent hooligans which, under the direction of political desperadoes, is evolving into a threat to public safety and security. The undisguised calls for violence at this rally and the resulting search for weapons, as well as the abuse against protesters present at the meeting, plainly reveal the nature of this movement which, having grown on Munich soil, has managed to expand and transfer its area of operation to Berlin.

But Berlin is not Munich. Just as we protected Berlin from the domination of communism, we will protect the people of Berlin from the terror of this hooligan-Socialist Workers' Party.[95] We will nip this movement in the bud, in Berlin and

---

[94] These are the locations of the headquarters of the SPD, the police department, and the KPD, respectively.

[95] In January 1919, there was an armed insurrection in Berlin known as the Spartacist uprising. It was fought between the SPD, with the Freikorps on their side, and the KPD. The SPD wanted a socialist democracy, while the KPD wanted a Soviet-style "republic." The revolt was suppressed after seven days with approximately 150 deaths, mostly among the insurgents.

throughout Prussia; it is accustomed to violence against those
who have a different opinion and strives to violate the law.

This is what the Minister President of Prussia, Otto Braun, wrote in
Berliner Morgenpost on Friday, May 6th, 1927. He was seriously mis-
taken. The movement was not nipped in the bud, not in Berlin and
not in Prussia. Despite the hate and the ban, its ideal rose ever higher!
Each instance of persecution only made the organization stronger
and firmer. No doubt many of us left, but these were only those who
were not strong enough for the challenges. A solid and unshakeable
core remained, and the Party itself survived despite its ban. The ideal
was too firmly anchored in the hearts of its faithful supporters for
anyone to hope to uproot it by force.

The National Socialist movement in Berlin was now put to the
test; it had to prove that its vitality was tenacious. It triumphed in a
heroic struggle, full of self-sacrifice, and thereby affirmed with its victorious advance the slogan under which it began: "Banned but not
dead!"

7. Smear Campaigns and Persecution

The victorious march of the young National Socialist movement in the capital of the Reich had come to a sudden halt after the police department pronounced a ban on the Party. The public life of the Party was reduced to nothing, the organization dislocated, activism brought to a halt, the band of fellow travelers scattered to the four winds, all direct contact between the leadership and the Party members broken off. The ban on the Party had been enforced with rigorous severity by the authorities. In fact, it had not been declared under the Act for the Protection of the Republic, and it therefore proved impossible to punish individual offenses with harsh fines and prison sentences. It was based on ordinary civil law dating from the time of Frederick the Great.[96] For carefully considered reasons, it was not motivated by political appeals but by criminal law. The ban had been proclaimed by the police, not by the ministry; it could thus be circumvented perhaps more easily and with less risk than a political ban, which is generally issued under threat of severe penalty.

By proceeding in this manner, the police department had already blatantly overstepped its powers. It had issued the ban for the city of Berlin *and* the province of Brandenburg, although it was clearly lacking any authority to do so, at least as regards Brandenburg. The chief

---

[96] Referring to the General State Laws for the Prussian States. The civil code served to bridge the gap between the old institutions of feudal law and the emerging requirements of capitalism. Thus, even when Goebbels had first authored this book, the laws were an antiquated relic, which reveals how desperate the authorities were at the time to ban the National Socialist movement in Berlin.

of police could at best ban the Party in Berlin; if to justify the ban it was alleged that the Party was guilty of illegal conduct, its ban could only be legally considered if the continued existence of the Party endangered public order and safety—assuming the allegations were true.

But they were simply untenable. Our activists had been attacked by political adversaries and had defended themselves. They had thus exercised the most basic right of every citizen: the right to self-defense. Our members had never been the attackers but only the victims. Nowhere could one speak of abuse on our part. We only used physical force to the extent that we were defending our lives.

Furthermore, no evidence could be produced that the Party itself had encouraged or taken responsibility for such action; the fact that a Party member defended himself when he had no other choice was clearly understandable and had nothing to do with the Party itself. The police department was more than likely fully aware of how legally tenuous their reasons for the ban were. We immediately filed an appeal with the *Oberpräsident* and subsequently with the administrative appellate court.[97] But the trial was postponed for years, as the police department continually requested postponements to produce the necessary evidence. It was only ruled upon long after the ban had been lifted. The administrative appellate court shirked from providing a clear ruling, which would likely have been ruinous for the police department; instead, they ruled that the ban had expired and that we thus lacked the legal standing to continue the lawsuit. The mere fact that the police department was incapable of providing the necessary evidence in court clearly indicated that the ban constituted a partisan act that had little to do with the impartial administration of law.

For the time being, however, the harassment against us continued. Efforts were being made to completely suppress the public activity of the Party and to rob it of its last financial means by dislocating its organization. We did not have any Party publications in Berlin at the time. Political efforts relied almost exclusively on mass meetings. Certainly, it was not possible, even by interpreting the statutes as broadly as possible, to forbid promoting any given political ideology in the capital of the Reich. It therefore remained possible to convene meetings, under assumed names, where National Socialism was discussed. In the beginning, that is what we did, but the police

---

[97] The *Oberpräsident* was the highest-ranking administrative official of the province, beginning from the time of the German Empire until 1947.

department quickly struck back and banned the meetings one after the other under the pretext that they disturbed public peace and order and should be regarded as a resumption of a banned organization.

It was decidedly arbitrary, but it served its purpose. This made it impossible to bring the concept of National Socialism into public discourse at all. The police intervened immediately if there was even the slightest mention of it.

Our next attempt hoped to have our representatives in the Reichstag speak to the voters of Berlin.[98] As for me specifically, I was absolutely forbidden from speaking in public. Members of Parliament from the Party soon took my place; mass meetings were organized, and our members of parliament spoke in my stead. The speakers commented on contemporary political issues, and they never failed to rebuke the Berlin police for their persecution of the National Socialist movement.

Personally, I was very deeply affected by this ban on speaking. I actually had no other means of maintaining the necessary contact with my Party comrades. We still lacked the press in which I could have expressed myself by writing. All meetings in which I wanted to speak were banned. When members of parliament were to appear in our meetings, these were also very frequently subject to injunctions announced at the last minute, and the activists that had remained faithful felt their anger and indignation steadily growing.

It was not the fact that we were persecuted, but the manner and methods by which the movement was suppressed and beaten down that had created an over-agitated atmosphere in our ranks, causing serious concerns. It seemed the police department was happy to ban our meetings only at the last minute, thus clearly hoping to deprive the Party of the possibility to inform its members of the ban in a reasonable time. Most of the time, there were hundreds and thousands of them responding to the invitation, and when they arrived to the venue, they were met with locked doors and a solid cordon of police officers.

---

[98] The Reichstag was the lower chamber of Germany's main legislature under the German Empire as well as Weimar Germany. In the Weimar system, the members of the Reichstag were directly elected by the people, akin to the members of the US House of Representatives or the members of the British House of Commons. Thus, this activity would in theory be the protected speech of legislative officials.

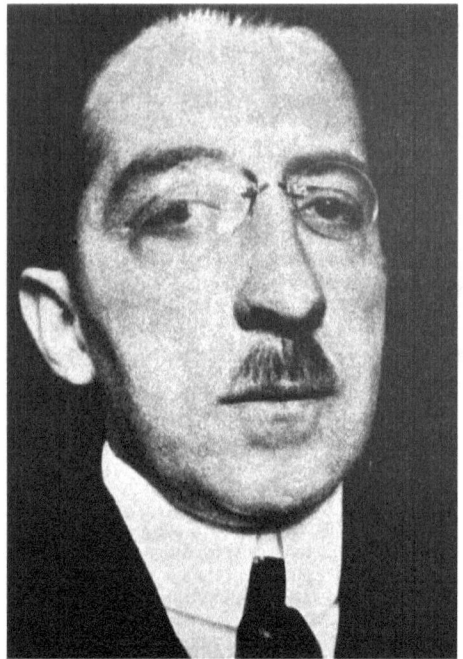

Dr. Bernhard Weiss, deputy chief of police in Berlin.

Just a few words say it all: "A life of beauty and dignity."

It thus became easy for snitches and bribed provocateurs to en-
rage the directionless and leaderless crowd and incite them to violence against the police and those with opposing political opinions.
Most often, small attack squads then separated themselves from the
indignant crowd and took pleasure in roaming the Kurfürstendamm
and giving vent to their anger by slapping and occasionally beating
the "innocent passer-by who looked Jewish."[99]
Of course, the press, with all its demagoguery, vehemently re-
proached the Party which, already being banned, had no possibility
of addressing its supporters in any way. The public then echoed the
cries and howls of Jewry. Throughout the country, they sought to
give the impression that in Berlin, in the midst of the most tranquil
peace, pogroms against the Jewish population were being organized,
evening after evening, as if the NSDAP had established a clandestine
headquarters from which these attacks were systematically guided.

This was the tone of the press:

Put an end to the Kurfürstendamm riots![100] It is impossible to
remain silent in the face of the brutal acts of violence of the
National Socialists on the Kurfürstendamm. This has become
the usual form of entertainment for these juvenile delinquents.
West Berlin is one of the prestigious districts of this city. Such
shameful and shocking scenes cause the most serious damage
to Berlin's reputation. As the preference of this swastika-clad
group for the Kurfürstendamm is now sufficiently known to
the police, it should not only crack down after the attacks, but
should take swift and severe precautionary measures when-
ever a meeting of National Socialist vandals is planned.

This is what the *Berliner Zeitung am Mittag* published on May 13th,
1927.[101]

---

[99] The Kurfürstendamm is a boulevard in western Berlin. Its development reached
its peak in the Weimar Republic in the 1920s, at which point it was a shopping and
entertainment center with an active nightlife.
[100] "The Kurfürstendamm Riots" is the name assigned to the so-called pogroms that
the National Socialists carried out against the Jews in Berlin. The most notable "riots" occurred in 1931 and again in 1935.
[101] Also known as the *B.Z. am Mittag*, the *Berliner Zeitung am Mittag* was one of many
tabloids owned by the Jew Leopold Ullstein's media conglomerate.

To the extent that there really were any "riots," it was the fault of the police department—and the police department alone. It had the power to let us contact our supporters, to calm them down, but because it took this option away from us, whether it wanted to or not, it provoked these incidents of political struggle, which were the logical consequence of such persecution.

Perhaps the police were glad that things were developing this way. The reasons to continue imposing the ban on the Party were insufficient in the people's mind, so they tried to manufacture a reason. The public had to point fingers at us. Their opinion had to be that this party was nothing more than a crowd of criminals, and that the authorities were only doing their duty by killing it off.

The National Socialist movement is based on meritocratic hierarchy more than any other party. For it, the Führer and his authority determine everything. It rests in the hands of the Führer to administer party discipline or to let it sink into anarchy. If we remove the leaders of the Party and we thus destroy the basis of authority that preserves the organization, we then decapitate the masses. Reckless behavior is always the consequence. We could no longer influence the masses. They became rebellious, and one should therefore not be surprised if they ended up engaging in violence.

As absurd as it may seem, those in power can only be thankful for the existence of the National Socialist movement. The anger and indignation about the consequences of the mindless reparations policy—which they had pursued since 1918—are so strong among the people that they would plunge Germany into a bloodbath in the shortest possible time, had they not been subdued and tamed by our movement. The National Socialist efforts did not drag our people into catastrophe, as the professional politicians behind this catastrophe would have us believe. We only spotted the catastrophe at the right time for the right reason, and we have never made a secret of our opinions on the lamentable state of Germany.

A catastrophe is not caused by the one who rightly calls it a catastrophe; on the contrary, it is caused by these catastrophic politicians. And no one could blame us for *that*. We have never participated in a coalition government. Since the birth of the movement, we had been in the opposition and fought the course of German politics as vigorously as possible. From the beginning, we predicted the consequences, the contours of which are now beginning to emerge more and more clearly on the political horizon.

Our observations were so natural and compelling that the masses welcomed them with ever-increasing sympathy. As long as we controlled the momentum of the people and led them with rigid discipline, there was no danger that their waves of rage would crash uncontrollably onto the existing regime. Undoubtedly, National Socialist campaigning was, and is, the voice for the national angst. But as long as that voice is allowed to speak, we can control the people's anger and thus ensure that it is expressed in a lawful and tolerable manner.

If one deprives the people of their representatives and the interpreters of their suffering, then one thus opens the door to anarchy, because we are not the ones who pronounce the most radical and uncompromising judgment on the ruling regime. It is the people. It is the common man who is not accustomed to mincing words, who does not hide his heart but expresses his growing rage in an ever more vivid form, who thinks more radically and more uncompromisingly than we do.

The National Socialist voice is a sort of safety valve for those in power. The indignation of the masses has an outlet through this valve. If it becomes blocked, anger and rage then flow back into the masses and rise to an uncontrollable boiling point.

Political criticism always attacks the failures of the system being criticized. If the failures are benign and if the good intentions of the person who commits them cannot be doubted, criticism will then be expressed in a fair-minded and civilized form. But if the failures are so pivotal that they threaten the very foundation of the state, and beyond that, if there is reason to suspect that those who are at fault do so, not with good intentions, but in bad faith, then the criticism will become all the more unbridled and bitter. Radical politics is directly proportional to radical abuse perpetrated by the ruling regime. If the regime's failures are so fatal that they threaten to ultimately plunge the people, the economy, or even the entire civilization of the country into an abyss, then the opposition can no longer content itself with criticizing the symptoms of the diseased state and demanding a remedy. It must, rather, attack the system itself. At this point, it is in fact "radical" to the extent that it seeks out the root causes of the failures and strives to eliminate them at their very roots.[102] Before

---

[102] Etymologically, "radical" comes from the Latin word *radix* meaning "root." In this sense, the National Socialist movement was truly radical as it sought to remedy the root causes of German society's decline.

Poster for a meeting under the ban:
"The National Socialist Reichstag Representative Hans Dietrich speaks...."

the Party was banned, we had firm control over our supporters. The police department had the ability to monitor the Party very carefully in its organization and activity. Any partisan mistake made in the heat of the moment could be immediately and directly punished. Now, after the ban, things were completely different. The Party no longer existed, its organization being dislocated. Its leaders could no longer be held responsible for what was happening since they had been cut off from their supporters. I was now a private citizen and had no intention of assuming responsibility for any of the unfortunate political events that the police department gave rise to through its ceaseless persecution of us. Moreover, the Jewish clique of tabloid journalists seemed to take particular pleasure in insulting me personally, when I no longer had any means of defending myself against their political and personal insults. It was certainly in the hope of alienating the masses—with whom I had lost all contact—from the movement and from me, thus leaving them prey to demagoguery, especially from communists.

For the first time, I experienced what it meant to be the beloved target of the Jewish press. There was absolutely nothing for which I had not been criticized, and yet their attacks were all made-up lies.

Of course, I had neither the desire nor the time to respond. The uninitiated often wonder why National Socialist leaders so rarely respond to Jewish slander with legal means. Surely, they think, we can demand the Jews make corrections in their papers, we can sue them for defamation, or have them prosecuted.

But that is easier said than done. In any given Berlin newspaper, one of these lies could appear, and then it makes its rounds through hundreds and hundreds of provincial newspapers that rely on it. Each of these provincial papers adds its own particular commentary, and if we begin to even try to make corrections to it, the end would never be in sight. This is precisely what the Jewish press wants, because the Jew, whom Schopenhauer described as the master of lies, never tires of lying.[103] No sooner have we corrected a piece of false news today than it is replaced the next day by another. If we go after the second lie, what is stopping those Jewish reptiles from fabricating a third one the day after tomorrow? Taking the matter to court? Are National Socialist leaders only there to argue with Jewish liars in front of a judge?

In any case, the public prosecutor refuses to intervene on our behalf, claiming a lack of public interest.[104] We are reduced to civil lawsuits, which cost a lot of time and even more money. To restore our reputation before the courts of the republic against these Jewish defamers, we would have to spend an entire life and a fortune.

A trial such as that takes at least six months, if not longer, at which point the public has long forgotten about the matter. The Jewish muckraker then simply claims in court that he has fallen victim to a mistake and usually gets off with a minimal fine. Of course, the publisher will gladly pay it for him. The next day, however, the same

---

[103] Arthur Schopenhauer was a German philosopher active in the early nineteenth century. In his work *Parerga and Paralipomena* (1851), Schopenhauer comments on the historically unfavorable sentiment toward the Jews: "We see also from the two Roman authors [Tacitus and Justinus] how much the Jews were at all times and by all nations loathed and despised. This may be due partly to the fact that they were the only people on earth who did not credit man with any existence beyond this life and were, therefore, regarded as cattle, as the dregs of humanity, as great masters at telling lies" (vol. 2, p. 357 (footnote) [Oxford: Oxford University Press, 2010]). For further information about Schopenhauer's comments on the Jews, please refer to *Eternal Strangers* by Thomas Dalton (Uckfield: Castle Hill Publishers, 2020).

[104] "Public interest" is a nebulous legal concept. In essence, it is a set of subjective criteria to determine whether a potential criminal offense ought to be prosecuted by the state. Here, the state refuses to criminally prosecute the libel because, it claims, it failed to meet those criteria.

newspaper publishes an article about the trial that leads the unknowing reader to believe that the Jewish liar was actually totally in the right, and that there must be some kernel of truth in the lie, otherwise the judge would not have let the defendant off with such a lenient penalty. And with that, the Jewish press would have truly achieved everything it wants to achieve. It first discredits and assassinates the character of the political opponent in public. It then steals his time and money with a lengthy trial. Next, it turns its defeat in court into a victory, and sometimes a judge who lacks instinct lets the liar go completely unpunished by pretending "legitimate interests" mitigated the libel.

These are not satisfactory ways of remedying defamation by the Jewish press. A man who leads a public life must be aware that if he attacks corrupt politicians, they very quickly defend themselves by sounding the alarm in public and replacing compelling objective evidence with personal defamation. This is why he must develop thick skin and become completely indifferent to Jewish lies, and maintain his cool, especially when he is preparing to strike with hard political blows. He must know that every time he puts the enemy in danger, the enemy will attack him personally. Then he will never experience unpleasant surprises. On the contrary, in the end, he will even be glad he was insulted and smeared by the scum of the press, because it is ultimately the surest sign that he is on the right path and that he has struck the enemy's weak point.

It was difficult even for me to accept this stoic point of view. In the early days of my work in Berlin, I had to suffer immensely from attacks in the press. I took all of it far too seriously and was often in despair that there was clearly no possibility of preserving my personal honor in the political struggle. That changed quite a bit over time. In particular, the excessive press attacks killed all my sensitivity to them. If I knew or suspected that the press was defaming me personally, I would not even touch a Jewish newspaper for weeks and thus kept cool, calm, and collected. If I read all the lies and nonsense a few weeks after it was first printed, it suddenly loses any significance it may have had. I then see how vain and useless all this fuss is, and above all I gradually build my ability to see past the press campaigns and uncover their ulterior motives.

There are only two ways to become famous in Germany today: either—if you will pardon my saying so—fellate the Jew's ego or fight him ruthlessly and relentlessly. While the former is only an option for the literati of democratic society and flip-flopping careerists, we National Socialists have settled on the latter. And our decision must be carried out to its logical conclusion. To this day, we have had no problems with our success. In his schizophrenic fear of our massive attacks, the Jew has entirely lost his calm composure. At the end of the day, he is nothing more than a foolish demon. People often overestimate, especially in circles of the German intelligentsia, the purported far-sightedness, shrewdness, and intellectual acumen of the Jew.

The Jew only ever assesses a situation clearly when he has complete control over it. If, for example, a political adversary unexpectedly confronts him with a harsh attitude, leaving him with the impression that this is a fight to the death, then the Jew immediately loses his sober composure. He is—and this is perhaps the chief trait of his character—deeply perturbed by the sense of his own inferiority. The Jew himself could be described as the very personification of a repressed inferiority complex. Hence, nothing can affect him more deeply than when he is recognized for who he truly is. Call him swine, scoundrel, liar, criminal, murderer, or killer; this will hardly bother him. But look him in the eye for a moment and then say to him, "You are just a Jew!" and you will be astonished at how insecure, embarrassed, and self-conscious he immediately becomes.

This also explains why prominent Jews consistently involve the authorities when anyone calls them Jewish. It would never occur to a German to take legal action if he were called German, because a German always feels proud of his ethnicity and never ashamed. The Jew, on the other hand, resorts to legal action when he is called a Jew, because he knows in the depths of his heart that this is something despicable and that there can be no worse insult.

We have never put much effort into countering Jewish defamation. We knew we were being defamed. We adapted to it in time and did not think it our duty to refute the lies one by one, but rather to undermine the credibility of these Jewish journalists.

And this we have achieved to the greatest extent over the years. If we ignore the lie, it soon dies off by itself. Out of desperation, the Jew ultimately fabricates lies and slanders so wild that even the most gullible oaf no longer believes them.

"They lie! They lie!" With this battle cry we confronted the barrage of Jewish filth. Here and there, we singled out a few individual lies from the confused heap of slander, which allowed us to clearly illustrate the nasty tricks of Jewish journalism. And so we said, "Do not believe anything they say! They lie, because they have to lie; they have to lie, because they have nothing else to say."

It is nauseatingly grotesque when a poorly scrawled Jewish paper claims to be morally obliged to scrutinize the private lives of National Socialist leaders in order to uncover some dirt on them. A race that bears the weighty guilt and responsibility for two millennia's worth of crime, especially against the German people, is truly in no position whatsoever to lecture the public on morality among civilized people. First of all, whether a National Socialist leader has made a mistake here or there is not even up for discussion. Rather, the only matter that remains is determining who led the German people into this indescribable misery and paved the way for this misery with catchy slogans and false promises, in the end only to watch with folded arms as an entire nation descends into chaos. When this question is answered and the culprits are brought to justice, then they can look into our flaws.

We cannot also ignore the spineless lack of principle that enables the bourgeois press to obsequiously yield to the shameless hypocrisy of the Jewish journalist mercenaries. The bourgeois press is always quick to help when it comes to smearing a nationalist politician or castigating the National Socialist press for alleged wrongdoing. When dealing with Jewish tabloid journalism, on the other hand, the bourgeois press is puzzlingly and irresponsibly lenient. They fear the caustic reporting and sheer ruthlessness of these tabloids. They clearly do not want to venture into the danger zone. They are filled with an overwhelming feeling of inferiority compared to the Jew, which forces them to try anything and everything to stay on his good side.

It ought to make the news in itself when the bourgeois press does on occasion muster the courage to speak a mild word of criticism against the Jewish liars. Most of the time, it prefers to limit itself to an "elegant silence" and says, "Anyone who handles filth becomes filthy in the process," as an excuse.

*　　*　　*

The fact that the Jewish press attacked and defamed us was not even the worst thing. We knew well that all these lies would sooner or later come crumbling down on them. When an idea is right, it is right, and can never be killed off with the lies of its enemies. The administrative decisions that fell swiftly upon the movement after the ban was announced affected us more gravely. The organization was destroyed, and maintaining its regular membership became impossible. This meant that the Party's most important financial source dried up. The rumor that the National Socialist movement lives off donations from bigwig capitalists is simply not true. We have not seen even a cent of the troves of money that the Pope, Mussolini, France, or Goldschmidt supposedly gave us.[105] The Party lived and still lives exclusively on the contributions of its members and the income from its meetings. If these sources of revenue dry up, the Party then loses any chance of survival.

This is exactly what happened after the ban. The moment members' regular contributions stopped and revenue from meetings no longer came in—most meetings had been forbidden, and those that were authorized generated no profit—the Party went through its worst financial crisis. It had to reduce its administrative functions to the bare minimum. Salaries were also cut to a minimum, and even then they could only be paid in installments of small sums. In response to these dire straits, Party officials adopted an admirable spirit of self-sacrifice; not a single one of them was let go, but all of them then gave up twenty, thirty, even fifty percent of their already meager salary, in order to keep the Party alive.

From time to time, the police department graciously allowed me the privilege of speaking at a public meeting. It gave me an opportunity to pour out my heavy heart, but this happened so rarely that the political value of such "generosity" was virtually non-existent.

When the police department, under pressure from the public, finally lifted its ban on us in Brandenburg—which, again, it lacked all authority to impose in the first place—the Party officials were at least

---

[105] i) The Pope for most of the time during the NSDAP's rise to power was Pius XI, who had emphasized Catholic social teaching including strong condemnations of communism and Marxist socialism. ii) Benito Mussolini had been the Fascist Prime Minister of Italy since 1922. iii) At the time, the Third Republic of France was dominated by the left-wing Radical Socialist party; however, the Dreyfus affair (beginning in 1894 until its nominal resolution in 1906) had left deep and lasting divisions in French society. The conservatives of France may have felt compelled to donate to the NSDAP after being on the "losing" side of the Dreyfus affair. iv) Jakob Goldschmidt was a wealthy Jewish banker who managed the large Danatbank and oversaw its subsequent failure and bankruptcy, which only contributed to the European banking crisis of 1931.

able to convene outside Berlin, most often in Potsdam, and discuss the most important matters of politics and organization.[106]

In Berlin, that remained completely out of the question. Not only were Party meetings banned but also those of all its subsidiary organizations. In fact, they even went so far as to ban a ceremony in Schlageter's memory, organized by the German Women's Order, a women's movement close to the NSDAP, for fear that it could "endanger public order and security."[107]

The inevitable consequence of banning such events was the increase of disorder on the streets. More than one Jew in western Berlin received a slap in the face for it. Although a random Jew was not personally to blame for what was done to the NSDAP, the masses simply do not care about these subtle distinctions. They take someone who is there, and even if Mr. Cohn or Mr. Krotoschiner from the Kurfürstendamm had no influence on the police department, in any case they belonged to that race, in any case they were a party, in any case the common man saw them guilty.[108]

Many SA men found themselves in prison at this time, as they were accused of rioting at the Kurfürstendamm late in the evening. The courts imposed draconian sentences. In most cases, a simple shove cost six to eight months in prison, but this truly was no way to prevent mischief. As long as the Party was banned and its leaders were deprived of the opportunity to mollify the masses, such misdeeds remained inevitable. The police department then inaugurated another policy that actually proved more harmful than all those tried until now. During major clashes, hundreds and hundreds of our activists were arrested for one reason or another, and transferred without explanation to the political crimes unit of the police department. Most of the time, they made no attempt to legally justify the arrest.

---

[106] In other words, the police department lifted the ban on the NSDAP for the province of Brandenburg but kept it in place for the city of Berlin itself, which is geographically located within Brandenburg but remains a separate political entity. Potsdam is the capital of Brandenburg, situated approximately twenty-five miles southwest of Berlin.

[107] Albert Leo Schlageter was a decorated German military officer who served in the First World War. He led resistance against the French after they occupied the Ruhr in 1923, for which he was promptly betrayed by his colleague and put to death. He was considered a martyr and hero for Germany by many nationalists. The German Women's Order was a nationalist women's association founded in 1926 that eventually evolved into the National Socialist Women's League.

[108] Cohn and Krotoschiner are stereotypical surnames for Jews in Germany.

They were crowded into holding cells and detained until noon the next day. They were then released without any punishment.

Prosecuting them seemed entirely unnecessary to the gentlemen at Alexanderplatz. They did not want to sentence the Party members and the SA men at all, but rather only create difficulties for them with their employers. The unfortunate political prisoner would miss half a day of work because of the arrest; at best, he could show up to work around 2 P.M. His Marxist supervisor would quickly discover why he was tardy, only for him to be immediately put out of a job. This was the ultimate goal of the arrests!

The arrest of a National Socialist "hardened criminal."

The Social Democratic Party, before the war, fought the spiked-helmet system with an exaggerated passion.[109] The spiked helmet was the first victim of the 1918 revolution. The Marxists exchanged it for police batons instead. A baton seems to be the main symbol of the Social Democratic Party. Under the reign of a police baton, we endure the indescribable coercion of opinion and the shackling of conscience. We National Socialists have experienced this first-hand. We were thus able to learn to distinguish theory from praxis, and we

---

[109] The spiked helmet (*Pickelhaube*) is headgear, typically associated with the Prussian Army, worn by German soldiers and police in the nineteenth and twentieth centuries. To the rabid Marxists, it represented the German monarchy and the "old" Germany, especially its values of order and discipline.

sometimes came to conclusions different from those that are found in the Weimar Constitution.[110]

Just as this was going on, a member of our party, a simple worker from Munich, Georg Hirschmann, minding his own business without provoking anyone, was knocked out in the middle of the street by thugs from the Reichsbanner and beaten with wooden boards, planks, and lead pipes for so long that he ended up dying alone and forsaken in some gutter.[111] And how did the bourgeois police department react to such a brutal act of violence? The Reichsbanner was left completely unscathed. The Marxist press smeared our murdered comrade with impunity, and a meeting organized by the National Socialist movement in protest against this murderous terror was banned by the police.

The bourgeois world collapsed under the terrible blows of Marxist terrorism, and it deserved no other end. But we were willing to break this terror. After witnessing and suffering all this, how can anyone judge us for becoming so bitter and hostile?

In these difficult weeks, the SA man was, as always, the champion of our cause. For the first time, he was forced to remove his revered brown uniform, his proud flags were rolled up, and Party insignia could no longer be worn. Discreetly we wore an inconspicuous *Wolfsangel* pin on the right lapel of our jackets.[112] Steadfast members recognized each other by this symbol. It escaped the eye of the law, was soon carried by thousands of people, and appeared more and more on the streets of the Reich's capital. Whoever wore the *Wolfsangel* thus expressed his desire to resist, proclaiming in front of everyone that he was, despite everything, willing to continue the fight. He provoked a hostile world and displayed his conviction that we would

---

[110] With a sarcastic understatement, Goebbels criticizes the Weimar system, and the Marxists and Social Democrats that ran it, for professing support for certain political values, such as freedom of conscience and support for liberal democracy (their "theory"), while hypocritically contradicting those values by brutally repressing their political opponents using state authorities (their "praxis"). As Goebbels saw it, all this flouted the Weimar Constitution and explains why National Socialists did not care about it at all.

[111] Georg Hirschmann was viciously assassinated in Munich on the night of May 26th, 1927.

[112] The *Wolfsangel* is a Z-shaped symbol, inspired by the Germanic wolf hook originally used to hunt wolves. Today, it is commonly associated with right-wing extremism.

ultimately win the clash between National Socialism and Jewish sub-humanity.

*   *   *

The more we were hounded by the hostile press and targeted by the police, the more ardent our desire became to defend ourselves against the lying journalists, even if only on a smaller scale. We were missing a newspaper. We were not allowed to talk, so now we would write. Our pen had to be put at the service of the organization; the broken contact between Party leadership and its base had to be restored. It was necessary to strengthen the faith of our members, at least once a week, to encourage them to persevere.

It was then that the idea of founding our own newspaper arose for the first time from our plight. Certainly, we knew that we could hardly oppose the great power of the Jewish press. Nonetheless, we started modestly, because we had to; because we believed in our strength.

Such a weekly publication had to, in keeping with the struggle in Berlin, be aggressive. It had to clear the way to the movement using the fiercest journalism. We wanted to match the Jewish press in caustic commentary and acerbic wit, with the only difference being that we stood for a great and pure cause.

We were stalked prey that the huntsman drove through the woods by shooting. When finally the prey has no other way out, it faces its pursuer, not only to defend itself, but to attack with its sharp teeth and antlers forward.

We were now determined to do so. We had been driven to despair. All means of defense had been taken away from us. We therefore had to turn against the pursuer, to build a solid position in retreat in order to then go on the offensive.

The title of our newly founded paper was obvious. It would be *Der Angriff*, with the subtitle: "For the oppressed! Against the oppressors!"[113]

---

[113] In English, the title translates to "The Attack."

8. Der Angriff

Publishing its own newspaper had become undeniably necessary for the banned Party of Berlin. Since the police department had suppressed all public action of the movement including meetings, posters, and demonstrations, there was nothing left for us to do other than gain new ground through the influence that the press has on the masses.

Even when the Party was not banned, we were already thinking about founding our own paper for the Berlin movement. But bringing this plan to fruition had always failed owing to a variety of obstacles. First of all, we lacked the funds to set up a press company that would meet the current needs of the movement. Then a number of difficulties related to the organization and the Party itself blocked the way for this project. Last but not least, we were so engaged with activism in meetings and demonstrations that we did not have the time to effectively and successfully work on this project.

But now the Party was banned. Our meetings were illegal, and there could absolutely be no question of street demonstrations. After the first press campaign was over, a general silence about us reigned over the newspapers. By passing us over in silence, it was hoped that the movement, the organization of which had been forcefully crushed, would be liquidated.

We wanted to remedy this bad situation with our own newspaper. It would above all be an informative paper for the public. We also wanted to have a voice; we wanted to represent a piece of public opinion. Our goal was to reconnect the link between the Party leadership and the members, which had been mercilessly cut by the police department's draconian ban.

Even choosing a name for the newspaper was a source of difficulty. Some members came up with the most aggressively militant names. They certainly honored the courage of their spiritual forefathers, but on the other hand they neglected any formulation of political doctrine and activism. It was clear to me that much of this newspaper's success depended on its name. Its worldview had to be captured in a single word.

To this day, I vividly remember that evening when we gathered in a small circle to think about the future title of our newspaper. Then it suddenly came to me like an epiphany. Our newspaper can only have one title: *Der Angriff!* This name was effective activism, and it actually encompassed everything we wanted and intended.

The Berlin leadership in 1927

The purpose of this newspaper was not to defend the movement. We had nothing left to defend; everything had been taken from us. It was necessary to lead the movement from the defensive to the offensive, to become combative and aggressive; in a word, we had to attack. This is why *Der Angriff* was the only possible title.

Using the press, we wanted to continue the activism that was forbidden to us openly. It was not our intention to create a newspaper in the proper sense, in some way replacing the daily news for our members. Our paper had its origins in opinion and should also be written in this sense.[114] Our goal was not merely to inform but to inspire, to ignite, to spur on.

The paper we founded was to act like a whip, so to speak, which draws forgetful sleepers from their slumber and chases them forward into unrelenting activism. Like its name, the paper's slogan was also a worldview. Next to the title, it read in large, attention-seeking letters: "For the oppressed! Against the oppressors!" Here, too, the full fighting spirit of our new paper was already on display. The worldview and scope of this paper were summed up in its title and slogan alone. For us, it was only a matter of filling this title and slogan with active political life.

The National Socialist press has its own style to which it is worth devoting a few words. In the words of Napoleon, the press is "the seventh great power," and since the time this was first uttered, its influence has expanded rather than diminished.[115] What immense strength lies within it! We noticed this especially during the Great War. In the years 1914 to 1918, the German press was almost scholarly and scientific in its objectivity, whereas the Entente's press indulged in unbridled and impudent demagoguery. With a systematic refinement, it poisoned all of the world's opinion against Germany; it was not objective but radically tendentious. The German press strived to provide objective articles and to inform its readers of major events in the World War to the best of its ability. The Entente press, on the other hand, was written for a specific purpose. Its aim was to strengthen the force of the fighting armies and to preserve the faith of the people at war with us in their just cause, and in the victory of civilization over the threat of German barbarism.

The German government and army command staff even had to put an end to defeatist journalism being brought to the frontline. In France and England, something like that would have been unthinkable. Their press, not subject to Party influence, fought with fanatical

---

[114] In other words, *Der Angriff* was not originally conceived as an informative newspaper of objective journalism but would focus more on political commentary and opinion pieces.

[115] Napoleon's statement appears to be spurious, as the details of his alleged comments vary from author to author. Some historians have him referring to Joseph Görres' *Rheinischer Merkur* (an eighteenth-century liberal newspaper in Koblenz) as "the fifth great power of Europe." Others quote him on the same subject as talking about the "sixth great power." Here, Goebbels expands it to all the press and has him calling it "the seventh great power."

resolution for the national cause. It was one of the most important factors in their final victory.

The newspapers of the Entente thus served propaganda more than information. For them, it was not so much a question of establishing the objective truth as it was of aggressively contributing to the war effort. The common man approved of such a conception; above all, it was good nourishment for the soldier, who risked his life in the trenches for the cause of the nation.

The Great War did not end for Germany on November 9, 1918.[116] It continued, but this time with new methods and on a new battlefield. It passed from the realm of armed conflict into that of a colossal political and economic struggle. The goal, however, remained the same: the coalition of enemy states worked toward the total annihilation of the German people. What was (and remains) terrible about this fate is that there are large influential parties in Germany who lend a hand to the Entente in this fiendish effort.

Those who face this impending doom do not have to express a scholarly, objective, and level-headed opinion on political events. They are focused on the events taking place around them. They need not have any qualms about leaving it to a later era to determine the historical truth. Their duty is to participate in the creation of historical realities, to the benefit and advantage of their people and their nation.

The National Socialist press is almost exclusively set aside for this purpose. It is written with activism in mind. It is aimed at the broad masses and wants to win them over to National Socialism. While the bourgeois press is content to convey more or less unbiased information, the National Socialist press also has a much larger and more decisive task. It draws political conclusions from the information; it does not leave it to the reader to form them to his own liking. The reader must actually be educated and influenced in the meaning and direction of its goals.

Thus, the National Socialist newspaper is only one element of the movement's activism. It has a strong political aim, and that is why it should not be confused with a news outlet or even a bourgeois publication. The reader of the National Socialist press must be strengthened in his conviction by reading the newspaper. He is influenced in a very effective and practical manner. It must proceed with precision,

---

[116] This date marks the abdication of Kaiser Wilhelm II, but fighting itself ended two days later with the Armistice of November 11th, 1918.

with poise, with purpose. All the reader's thoughts and sensibilities must be drawn in a specific direction. Just as the orator has only the task of winning the listener to the National Socialist cause with his speech, so the journalist has only the task of achieving the same with his pen.

This was unprecedented in the entire German press, and was therefore very often misunderstood, opposed, or even ridiculed from the start. The National Socialist press, following its nature, did not have the ambition to compete with the major bourgeois or Jewish papers, regarding precision of reporting and the breadth of subjects to be covered. A worldview is always one-sided. Anyone who can consider a matter from two sides thereby loses his certainty and his rigor of judgment. The "pig-headed stubbornness" of our public action, for which we are so often criticized, is ultimately the secret of our victory. The people want clear and unequivocal decisions. The common man hates nothing more than ambiguity and the "both this and that" point of view. The masses think in a simple and crude manner. They like to simplify complicated facts and draw their clear and uncompromising conclusions from this simplification. Although their conclusions are most often simple and unsophisticated, they often find exactly the right answer.

Political activism that is founded on these observations will always touch the soul of the people where it is needed most. If it does not know how to make sense of the confusing facts, but rather if it merely takes the complexity of things at face value and reports that to the people, then it will fail to understand the common man.

The Jewish press is also not without its bias. Today, it can afford to openly display its opinions, because these are already widespread among the public and therefore no longer need to be defended with propaganda.

The highbrow Jewish papers are objective and appear to apply a sober dispassion as long as the power of Jewry remains secure. But this sober dispassion has so little to do with the true nature of the Jewish press—a fact that can always be seen when this power comes under threat. Then these bought-and-paid-for writers in the newsrooms lose all composure, and these serious journalists suddenly become the most deceitful scoundrels for a slanderous Jewish newspaper.

Of course, in the beginning we neither wanted to nor could we compete with the large Jewish papers, especially regarding the sheer volume of information. Those Jewish hacks were too far ahead. We did not have the desire to inform without campaigning; we wanted to fight and campaign. Everything is tendentious with National Socialism. Everything is geared toward a specific aim, toward a precise goal. Everything should serve this aim and goal, and everything that cannot serve it is unceremoniously eliminated without further ado. The National Socialist movement was made by great orators, not by great writers. It has this characteristic in common with all the decisive revolutionary movements in world history. From the outset, it had to subordinate its press to its doctrine. The press generally had to be edited by activists of the written word, just as the public action of the Party was organized by activists of the spoken word.

However, for us at the time, that was easier said than done. We certainly had a sizeable body of well-trained and efficient activists. Our best speakers came from the ranks of the movement itself. They had learned to speak publicly in the movement and for the movement. The technique of modern mass influence through posters and leaflets was impressively mastered by Party activists. But now it was time to transfer this art to the field of journalism.

The movement had only one mentor in this: Marxism. Before the war, Marxism had educated its press in the sense described above. The Marxist press has never had an informative character, only a tendentious one. Marxist editorials are written speeches. The entire presentation of the red press is consciously focused on influencing the masses. This is one of the great secrets of the ascent of Marxism. The leaders of the Social Democrats, who, after a struggle of forty years, made their party powerful and respected, were above all propagandists and remained so especially when they took up the pen. They never did simple office work. They were obsessed with the ambition to act for the masses, from the masses.

Even back then, we were no stranger to these observations. We had prepared for our difficult task. The new demands of our work consisted simply of putting theoretical principles into practice.

*   *   *

And even this could only be done to a modest extent at first. Before we could move on to actual activism, we had to clear the way of a number of material difficulties, which were taking up all our time and energy back then.

It is not difficult to start a newspaper when there is unlimited financing. Then, the best writers and publishing experts are available, and the business is practically guaranteed to succeed. It is more difficult to venture into the operation without funding while relying only on an organization, because what is missing in financing can then be replaced and compensated for by the inner rigor and solidarity of such an organization. But the most difficult thing is to establish a newspaper without funding and without an organization. Then, all that matters is the effectiveness of the paper, and the intelligence of those who write for it is critical to its success.

We had no funds for our newly founded paper. Who would be crazy enough to give money to us, this ridiculous little group that was banned and lacked any kind of support from either the authorities or the public?

They could kiss any money lent to us goodbye. We were not backed by a strictly disciplined organization, filled with a spirit of solidarity. Our party had been dislocated by a strict ban just as we were going to start the paper. So we had to resort to this desperate attempt to make our newspaper spring from the ground, so to speak—without money and without a solid following. I admit today that we were not at all aware of the difficulties of this task. Our plan was the result of our daring foolhardiness; we went ahead with it convinced that we basically had nothing left to lose.

But the name alone hit a bulls-eye. The newspaper's publicity launch made promising beginnings for the young company. In the last week of June, mysterious posters appeared on the bulletin boards of Berlin, and many people racked their brains over them. We had kept our plan as secret as possible, and we actually succeeded in hiding it entirely from the public eye.

Berlin was greatly astonished when one morning blood-red posters appeared with the pithy message: *Der Angriff!* People were interested when, a few days later, a second poster cropped up in which the mysterious insinuation of the first was certainly expanded upon, yet it refused to provide the uninitiated with a solution to the enigma. This second poster read, "*Der Angriff* launches July 4th."

It was a happy coincidence that, on the same day, the *Rote Hilfe* put up their own poster which read in menacing red letters that in the event of an accident and injury, one should immediately go to the local medical station of this communist aid organization.[117]

This exposed the insidious secret hidden behind these mysterious insinuations to the public. It was evident that the phrase *Der Angriff* referred to a communist revolt.[118] This coup was to begin on July 4th in Berlin, and as the poster from the *Rote Hilfe* proved, the KPD was already ensuring proper care and medical attention for the expected casualties.

This rumor spread like wildfire through the Reich's capital. It was taken up by the press, which could not help but speculate about it. The provincial press stammered in fearful bewilderment. In the *Landtag*, the politically centrist parties launched an investigation into any information about the impending communist coup that the government was willing and able to share. In short, there was great confusion everywhere. After two days, our third and final poster appeared, making it known that *Der Angriff* "was a Berlin-based German paper" published weekly and that it would be written "for the oppressed, against the oppressors!"

With this effective advertising technique, we had managed to make the name of the newspaper known before it had even been published. Obtaining the modest, yet all the more necessary, funds to establish the paper was more difficult. No one lent a single penny to the Party. I ended up borrowing the sum of two thousand marks, for which I was privately responsible. This sum was to ensure the beginnings of the new company. Today it seems ridiculous to mention such a small amount of money, but at the time, it meant a real fortune to us. For days, I had to run from place to place to raise funding with kind words and appeals to friends of the Party.

The first small group of subscribers was made up of Party members who still remained loyal. They participated in the promotional advertising of the newspaper with unflagging enthusiasm. Each activist was convinced that this was the most important task of the moment and that the survival of our movement in the capital of the Reich depended on its success.

Selling the paper on the street was entrusted to unemployed SA men, while its printing and publication was entrusted to a sympathetic firm, and we then set to work.

---

[117] The *Rote Hilfe* was a German aid organization closely associated with the KPD; it was active from 1924 to 1936.

[118] *Der Angriff* literally means "the attack" or "the raid" in English.

Advertisements before Der Angriff *was first published.*

The greatest difficulty lay in establishing a suitable editorial board. The movement had virtually no journalistic past. It had in its ranks good organizers and the best orators of the time, but it lacked writers or even simple professional journalists. As a last resort, it became necessary to simply engage Party members to do so. They showed a lot of goodwill, and some of them also had an ability to write, but they lacked real experience as journalists. When I first considered starting a newspaper, I counted on someone to be our editor-in-chief. I had managed to win him over to our project, but just as it was about to take shape, he was arrested for an old violation of the press laws and jailed in Moabit for two months.[119]

We were off to a bad start. None of us knew the press business or even knew enough to make the best of the situation. The layout of a newspaper, the technical preliminary tasks of each issue, proof-reading in and of itself—all this was a mystery to us. We truly approached this endeavor without the slightest technical knowledge, and it was a stroke of luck that allowed us to get away with it without any serious embarrassment.

*   *   *

We were more aware of the style and alignment we intended to give our newspaper. We knew exactly what we wanted, and there was virtually no conflict among us about it. That the face of the newspaper had to be absolutely new and symbolize the awakening young Germany was obvious. *Der Angriff* had to maintain a combative and aggressive character, and its presentation, its style, its method had to adapt to the nature and spirit of the movement.

The newspaper was written for the people. It therefore had to use their language. It was not our intention to create a paper for the "intellectual reader." *Der Angriff* was to be read by the masses, and they would only read what they understood.

Know-it-alls have sometimes criticized us for being witless and uncultured. They turned up their noses at the lack of intellectualism, which characterized our journalistic output, and compared it to the supposed intellectual refinement with which bourgeois papers, especially Jewish ones, were written. These reproaches hardly affected us. For us, it was not a question of imitating a false and misleading obsession with "culture." We wanted to win over the masses; we wanted to speak to the heart of the common man. We wanted to empathize with his thoughts and gain his support for our political ideal. As our success later demonstrated, we managed to do so to a large extent.

---

[119] Moabit is a neighborhood in central Berlin. The criminal court of Berlin and its jail is located there.

When we started in July 1927 with a circulation of two to three thousand copies, there were then large Jewish papers in Berlin with a circulation of one hundred thousand or more. They did not consider us worthy of any attention. Today, when our newspaper enjoys an impressive reach, these papers have long been forgotten. And yet they were so intellectually, so verbosely written that the reader got headaches from them! These literary hacks shone vainly and smugly in the dazzling complication of their intellectualism; they refined themselves into such a cultured style, to such an out-of-touch point, that the masses could no longer understand them.

We have never made these mistakes. We were straightforward, because the people are straightforward. We thought candidly, because the people think candidly. We were aggressive, because the people are not afraid to be aggressive. We consciously wrote in the way the people feel, not to flatter or pander to them but to gradually win them over to our side by speaking their own language and to systematically convince them of the merits of our politics and the harmful nature of our adversaries.

Three intrinsic characteristics distinguished our young paper from all the newspapers previously published in Berlin: a new kind of political editorial, a new kind of political weekly review, and a new kind of political cartoon.

For us, the political editorial was a written poster, or better yet, a street sermon transcribed on paper. It was short, energetic, designed for activism, and effective at it. It presumed precisely what we wanted to convince the reader of was true, and it drew our conclusions from it unperturbed. It was aimed at the general public and was written in a style that the reader could not fail to notice. Most of the time, the editorial of a bourgeois or Jewish newspaper is not read by the public. The common man believes that it is reserved for the elite intelligentsia. For us, however, the editorial was the heart of the entire newspaper. It was written in the language of the people, and right from the first sentence, it was so engaging that no one who began to read could put it aside without finishing it.

The reader should get the impression that the author of the editorial was in fact an orator who stood next to him, and wanted to convert him to his opinion with clear and convincing thought. The decisive concept was that this editorial provided the actual outline of the entire newspaper, according to which all the other articles were organically grouped. The entire issue thus had a fixed center of interest, and the reader was reinforced and hardened in this trend with every page.

The weekly review summarized the political events that had taken place during the week, but linked and subordinated them to the editorial. The facts were reported in a concise manner, and the political consequences were drawn from them with consistent logic and intellectual rigor.

Looking back at it, it was certainly somewhat monotonous, but was still effective in practice. We also understood that our task was less to produce large print runs than to present a few major guiding political principles, to formulate a few major political demands and to repeat them to readers in a hundred different ways without ever tiring.

To all this was added a completely new style of political cartoon. Under the constraints of the laws, it was almost impossible to express in words what we wanted and demanded. Speech provides clearly outlined facts that are easily subject to legal sanctions. It is different with political cartoons. They are open to numerous interpretations. It is possible to hide behind them at will. What one individual reads there is his own doing. The public is also more inclined to forgive an artist than a writer. The drawing pencil appears more challenging to the readership and therefore more admirable than the pen. Therefore, one shows greater sympathy toward the artist. Political caricature tends, depending on its nature, toward grotesque, ironic, and sometimes cynical effects. It more easily arouses laughter than it stimulates thought. And as we all know, those who have the laughs on their side are always right.

We did not fail to take advantage of this. Where we were forbidden to speak with the pen, we spoke with the drawing pencil. Typical representatives of democracy, who were overly sensitive to the mildest article published about them, were thrown to the lions before an eager public via merciless caricatures. A favorable coincidence had given us an outstanding political cartoonist. He combined effective political slogans with gifted artistic skill, bringing about caricatures that were undeniably hilarious.

In each issue, we attacked the prominent adversaries of our movement in Berlin, especially the deputy chief of police, Dr. Bernhard Weiss. This was done most of the time with such witty and blatant audacity that the subject of the cartoon found it absolutely impossible to react, even if the law was on his side. If he pursued legal recourse, he would inevitably have been ridiculed as a killjoy and sniveler. Our readers quickly got used to this genre and soon waited eagerly every Saturday for what *Der Angriff* would have in store this time for the powerful residents of Alexanderplatz.

The editorial, the weekly review, the political cartoon, and the other journalistic accoutrements as a whole brought coherence to the paper's activism efforts with overwhelming success. The newspaper thus achieved its original goal. It replaced, as far as possible, the spoken word. It perfectly restored the broken contact between Party leadership and its base; it re-established a solid bond of camaraderie throughout the Party, and gave each member the conviction that the cause was not lost, but that we had only changed tactics to defend it.

* * *

Obviously, it took quite a while before this result was achieved. We were just starting out and had to overcome a number of technical difficulties, which engaged all our time and energy. With the editor-in-chief selected for the newspaper still in jail, I promptly appointed our political secretary to serve that function for the new company. Although he had only a vague idea of the work that awaited him, he brought to his new position a sound mind and a certain amount of natural ability. First, he had to become familiar with the project. It was all the more difficult and duty-laden as the results of his work were under the close observation of a large audience; the paper was read not only by kindly friends, but also by enemies in bitter skepticism and arrogant superiority. The layout of our first issue was quite a task. None of us knew anything about it, and we all relied on each other. Time was running out, and we found ourselves faced with an impossible task.

One Monday morning, as I returned from a brief trip to the Sudetenland,[120] I found the first issue of the freshly published *Der Angriff* at a kiosk in the Hirschberg train station.[121] Shame, discouragement, and despair overwhelmed me as I compared this stopgap product to what I had actually wanted. A local rag, literal trash—those

---

[120] The Sudetenland is a region in the northwest of the modern Czech Republic that today borders Germany. At the time (in 1927), it was a region in Czechoslovakia with a heavy concentration of ethnic Germans.

[121] Hirschberg is a small town in Thuringia, approximately twenty-five miles from the border of the Sudetenland.

were my thoughts at first glance. Lots of enthusiasm but little skill—
those were my thoughts after giving it a quick read.

And most of our supporters and readers agreed with me. Much
had been promised, but little had been delivered. Most of us were
ready to throw in the towel and give up the project for good. But
with a final burst of effort, we pulled ourselves together. We did not
want to give our enemy the pleasure of seeing us at long last sink and
capitulate under his blows.

As soon as I noticed that a certain current of reluctance was swell-
ing within the movement, that our own members were discouraged
and despairing of the work, I decided to throw the last of my energy
into the fight. At a *Gau* rally convened in Potsdam at the last minute,
I addressed my comrades and explained in detail the principles underlying the aim and objective of our enterprise. I tried to make the
members understand that it was unbefitting of a National Socialist to
despair over a momentary failure, or to abandon a good cause just
because it became difficult. I did not fail to emphasize that if we began to doubt it, it would mean the end of the National Socialist movement in Berlin and the loss of all the ground conquered so far; an
immense responsibility rested on our shoulders, and everyone had to
think carefully before shirking this responsibility like a coward. The
effect of my speech on them was immediate.

With new courage, all the members went back to work. Admittedly, we launched our newspaper at an extremely unfavorable time;
the first issue was released in the middle of summer, on July 4th. The
organization was paralyzed, funds were lacking, a permanent editorial
board had not yet been formed, and our skills in journalism still left
much to be desired. But in the end, as always in hopeless situations,
our dogged determination and indomitable spirit guided us.

We had the will for it! That would be enough. The task we under-
took was necessary. That would be enough. Opposition can always
be overcome, if one has the will to do so. But a movement like ours
must never allow itself to be deterred when faced with opposition.
The beginnings of the new company were immediately threatened
with bankruptcy and collapse, but we bravely faced it. Diligence, hard
work, persistence, and talent also enabled us to overcome these difficulties. *Der Angriff* quickly justified its title and became a real attack.
Through tireless labor, this poor local rag was transformed in a very
short time into a formidable and impressive journal. We were getting
ever closer to the end goal. We were attacking. And from then on,

the young paper with its new face was to cause more headaches for those it targeted, rather than for us!

First issue of Der Angriff

9. Despair and Decline

In the meantime, we had reached the height of summer, and the off season was upon us. The political life of the Reich's capital was becoming duller and duller and losing its vigor. The Reichstag had gone on vacation. No major political surprises were to be expected anytime soon. The National Socialist movement in the city had seemingly collapsed, and there was not the slightest mention of it either in the press or elsewhere in public.

The defeatist elements who had infiltrated the movement took advantage of this to corrode and exhaust our efforts. Our newly founded paper was still in its preliminary stages, and as such did not yet meet the justified demands and wishes of the Party. The ban had reduced the Party's public audience to a minimum. Our membership records were incomplete and had to be maintained in secret, making the collection of membership dues very difficult.

The Party eked out a wretched existence. It lacked the funds necessary for political activity; it had no private donors, any more then than today, and we certainly could not donate from our own pockets as we were all poor. The little money that remained available to any given individual was squandered soon after the ban.

Among the members of the Party themselves, a growing dissatisfaction was emerging, systematically fueled and inflamed by provocative elements. The movement was kept in permanent anxiety and agitated by an insidious effort of demoralization as well as incessantly circulated alarmist rumors.

We could only publicly defend ourselves to a limited extent. We obviously had every interest in shielding as much as possible the internal life of the Party that continued to exist, even after its ban, from the eyes of the police, since we had to fear that, if it became visible, the authorities would rigorously intervene against us and the Party.

The administrative structure of the movement rested, once again, almost exclusively on the individual units of the SA. The Party was not so solidly structured and cohesive that it could engage in clandestine political action. However, the SA, at least in its more experienced units, had remained completely intact. Sometimes camouflaging them under the most curious names, active clubs were created where the National Socialist ideal was maintained, where the work continued as best as possible under the ban.

Savings associations were named "The Golden Penny," and bowling clubs, "The Good Wood," and swim teams, "The Water Wackos," and other whimsical names for groups that really only served to perpetuate the National Socialist movement, which had been unjustly dissolved by the police department.

Obviously, only carefully selected and completely trustworthy Party members could be employed for this task. The danger of moles and infiltrators was all too obvious. As soon as our activity went beyond a very limited circle of certain individuals, it inevitably came to the attention of the authorities, and was immediately subject to repression and harassment. All of our carping critics now thought it was their time to shine. They believed they had to let their voices be heard regarding how the Party leadership adapted under the pressure of the ban. They felt safe, considering that the Party had no way of taking action against them or their defeatist tendencies. In fact, we had to bite our lips and save our reprisals for a better day, as we watched rebellious Party members—and to a greater extent paid infiltrators—freely sabotage the Party.

In such a climate, our spirit of initiative, which had already been essentially paralyzed by police repression, sank into a pit. As soon as a decision was made, it was torn apart and chewed up by ill-willed individuals, and most often, all that resulted was a sterile and fruitless argument. If, however, nothing was done, these people would sadistically declare that the Party was crippled, and that there could no longer be any mention of a National Socialist movement in the capital city.

Der Angriff was also causing us great concern. As quickly as we overcame the initial technical difficulties, it was all the more difficult to overcome the financial difficulties. We founded the newspaper without any financial support. Our only investors were our own determination and desperation. From the outset, the company found itself threatened with the most serious hurdles. Our lofty ambitions were fulfilled only minimally. After a sudden but brief success at launch, public interest in our journalism quickly withered away, and as it was not possible to circulate our paper beyond our own circles, even the firm believers soon lost all confidence in this endeavor. The matter was considered hopeless. Our critics pontificated that we had been insufficiently prepared, that we should have waited until the fall, thereby not exposing ourselves to the danger of political torpor during the offseason in summer.

The number of regular subscribers was woefully inadequate; street vendors only sold a very small number of copies, which were published every Saturday evening. Because we were not able to generate the necessary revenue, we had to go into debt with our printer, and as a result the production of the newspaper, and its reputation, suffered. The paper was bad, and the printing was poor. *Der Angriff* became a third-rate leaflet appearing anywhere, anonymous and obscure, permanently deprived of the chance of ever being a major newspaper in the capital of the Reich.

After barely a month, *Der Angriff* was objectively on the verge of bankruptcy. Only the fact that we somehow managed to recover a small sum of money here and there at the last moment saved us from total bankruptcy.

All our time and energy was consumed by financial worries. Money, money, and money again! We could not pay for the printer. Salaries were only paid in small installments. We owed money for our rent and phone bills. The movement seemed to be suffocating under financial calamity.

If only at least we still had the possibility of organizing public meetings and influencing the masses with great orators! Perhaps that would help us overcome the looming financial crisis, because our meetings always brought in significant income, which had been our main source of income until now. But meetings were prohibited in general, and where they seemed authorized, the authorities required us to undertake costly preparations, only to slap the meeting with a sudden ban at the last minute. Then, we lost not only the expected revenue, but also the funds that we had spent to prepare for the meeting.

Very often the question has been raised in public as to where the National Socialist movement gets the funds necessary to maintain its large party apparatus and finance the extensive activism. People have suspected many different secret funds. Sometimes it was Mussolini, sometimes the Pope, sometimes France, sometimes Big Industry, and sometimes a famous yet unnamed Jewish banker—and all of them have financed the National Socialist movement! The most inane and absurd suspicions were raised in order to compromise the movement. The Party's worst enemies were cited as its most generous donors, and the masses were for years simply blind dupes of these fairy tales.

And yet nothing is clearer: the National Socialist movement has never received money from men and organizations outside its ranks, let alone those who publicly fought against the movement and were attacked by it. We never needed it anyway. The National Socialist movement is so large and vibrant that it can finance itself through its own means. From the dues alone, a party with a few hundred thousand members, today nearly a million, has a healthy financial base. It can thus, if it is administered judiciously, maintain its entire administrative apparatus—and for us this is a given. But the activism campaigns that we organize during elections or major political actions are self-financed.

This has been quite difficult for the public to understand, because other parties, to which we are often compared, are not at all in a position to charge an entry fee to their rallies. They are only too happy to fill their rooms by advertising free admission and even promising free drinks. This arises from the fact that, on the one hand, these parties only have mediocre speakers, and on the other hand, that the political values represented in their meetings do not attract or appeal to the broad masses.

It is different with the National Socialist movement. It has a group of speakers who can truly be said to be, by far, the best and most effective in Germany today. We did not systematically send these orators to school to train them into great rhetoricians; they sprang from the movement itself. Their inner zeal gave them the strength and power to stir the masses.

The people know if a speaker believes what he himself says. Our movement came from nothing, and the men who placed themselves at its disposal very early on were imbued with a just and necessary political ideal for which they advocated with blind conviction. They believe what they say, and through the power of speech, they pass on this conviction to their listeners.

The political speaker has usually never been at home in Germany. While Western democracies had very early on invented and refined the art of political speech for the people, in Germany itself, up until the end of the war, the political orator saw his activity limited almost exclusively to parliamentary debates. With our country, politics has never been the business of the people, but only the occupation of a privileged ruling class.

With the rise of the National Socialist movement, this all was to change. It was not Marxism that, strictly speaking, politicized the masses. Certainly the people came of age under the Weimar Constitution, but nothing was done to provide the possibility of true political action for the people during this time. The fact that, after the war, there were no meeting rooms where large crowds could be brought in to learn about political issues was already proof that the fathers of democracy did not seriously intend to educate the people politically. Rather, they saw the masses as mere electoral cattle, only fit to cast a vote in the ballot box but otherwise *misera plebs*, to be kept as far away as possible from the real problems of public life.[122]

The National Socialist movement was the origin, in many respects, of a notable transformation. Through its activism, it addressed the masses themselves, and it succeeded, after years of struggle, in putting a seriously frozen German political life back into motion. It invented a completely new language for political activism, and was able to popularize the problems of post-war German politics in such a way that the common man also understood and was interested in them.

Our activism has often been considered primitive and witless. But this harsh criticism was based on inaccurate assumptions. Certainly, National Socialist activism is simple, but it is also true that the people think in simple terms. Our activism simplifies the problems, and it consciously strips them of their confusing trappings in order to fit them into the people's perspective. When the masses recognized that

---

[122] *Misera plebs* is a Latin term meaning "the wretched masses." It, as Goebbels explains, implies the people lack both education and political training and should take no interest whatsoever in the essential problems of national life. They only mattered for the taxes they paid.

the pressing issues of the day were being dealt with in National Socialist meetings in a style and language that everyone could understand, tens and hundreds of thousands of attendees then flocked endlessly to our meetings. The common man found enlightenment, encouragement, hope, and faith there. He found there a solid point of support to which he could cling in the chaos of post-war confusion. He was thus ready to sacrifice his last penny for this movement. Only the awakening of the masses—he must be convinced of this—could lead to the awakening of the nation.

This explains why our meetings very quickly surged in popularity, and why the Party not only did not need to spend money on them, but turned them into the best and most enduring source of income.

The authorities struck us at our most vulnerable point when they banned well-known National Socialist speakers from making public speeches, including the leader of the movement himself, sometimes for months and years. They knew the enormous influence these men had on the masses. They were aware that the masses picked up and ran with the enthusiasm that these men brought into their speeches and that the movement received an impetus like absolutely no other from them.

The Berlin police, after issuing the ban, therefore aimed to make our movement's activism completely impossible. And that was the hardest blow we could ever take. We thus not only lost contact with the masses, but our most important financial source was artificially dried up.

Of course, we constantly tried to resume our activism in different covert ways. This worked once or twice, then one day the authorities discovered the trick and the bans came down again. In a modern democracy, the constitution plays only a secondary role in police tactics. In general, democracies are not too fastidious with their own written laws. Freedom of speech is hardly protected unless the opinion agrees with those of the government and the political parties supporting it. But when a lowly citizen dares to express an idea other than the officially endorsed opinion, freedom of speech is ignored, and coercion of speech and censorship appear in its place.[123] Of course, the victim can appeal to the constitution, but he risks receiving only a derisive laugh in response. The rights enshrined in the

---

[123] We see this happening even to this day in any number of liberal Western democracies. Today, the pretext of choice is to counter disinformation and to protect the so-called democratic institutions of the state.

constitution exist only for those who established it, and its obligations exist only for those against whom it was imagined.

Our gatherings were banned under any number of pretexts. National Socialist representatives in the Reichstag were even forbidden from speaking to their constituents. They did not hesitate to shamelessly cite an outdated law from the time of Frederick the Great, and thus called on Prussia, which was supposedly completely overthrown by the revolt of November 9th, 1918, to be their henchman.[124]

At that time, we still lacked the means to compensate for these bans using the press. The genre of *Der Angriff* was still too new for the masses to readily accept it. It was just starting out. The substance of this young newspaper was still so weakly crystallized that the potential for wide-ranging influence was totally ruled out for the time being.

Even within our own party, *Der Angriff* was the subject of much criticism. People found it too harsh, too radical, too impassioned. Its aggressive approach was too emotional and blustering for the halfhearted. It had not yet discovered how to win the hearts of its readers and was accomplishing little.

In fact, that in itself was a problem that caused us little concern. We could get by with hard work and diligence. Worse, however, was another difficulty that sometimes led the Party into serious danger, which, like any other crisis, was beginning to appear at the worst time.

The National Socialist movement in Germany basically has no predecessor. Certainly, it is linked through its demands and its doctrine to one or another cultural or political movement of the past. Its socialism is similar to that of Stoecker.[125] In its anti-Semitic tendencies, it is based on the preliminary work of Dühring, Lagarde, and Fritsch.[126] Its racial and cultural program is crucially and decisively influenced by Chamberlain's foundational insights.[127]

But the NSDAP did not just blindly and uncritically take up the results of this work to concoct a nebulous ideology from them. They

---

[124] Frederick the Great was the King of Prussia from 1740 to 1786.

[125] Adolf Stoecker was a German nationalist religious leader in the nineteenth century and founder of the Christian Social Party.

[126] Eugen Dühring was a German philosopher and economist; he was a vehement critic of Marxism and Jewry. Paul de Lagarde was a German professor who was strongly conservative and vocally opposed Jewry. Theodor Fritsch was a German journalist and publisher who often wrote critically of Jewry.

[127] A fervent admirer of Arthur de Gobineau, Houston Stewart Chamberlain was a British-German philosopher and author of *The Foundations of the Nineteenth Century*.

have been recast and brought into our intellectual and doctrinal work, and the essence of this process is that the National Socialist doctrine has synthesized this entire body of intellectual heritage into a comprehensive ideology.

The true National Socialist never likes to point out that he was involved in this or that pre-war movement that bears a distant resemblance to our party today. The National Socialist is a completely modern political type, and he recognizes himself as such. His essence is determined by the explosive revolutionary developments of the war and the post-war period.

Nevertheless, certain nationalist elements continue to haunt the ranks of the Party, imagining themselves to be the true spiritual fathers of the entire National Socialist worldview. They have made some part of our intellectual world their obsession, and believe that the Party is there only to use all its strength and activism in the pursuit of this obsession.

As long as the Party is engaged in major political tasks, these vague desires are perfectly harmless to its development. They become dangerous as soon as the Party enters into crisis following bans and internal difficulties. Specialists, interested *only* in the Jewish question or *only* in the racial question, then grant themselves full freedom of action.

They try very hard to misappropriate the work of the Party for their sometimes extraordinarily amusing specialties. They demand that Party leaders devote all the strength of the organization to their very specific interests. And if they refuse, most of the time they become the most bitter adversaries, just as before they were the most enthusiastic supporters, and launch into impetuous and unbridled attacks against the Party and its public activity.

Barely had the ban come down and the political activity of the movement suppressed when these nomadic apostles of nationalism appeared in droves. One advocated for the reform of the German language, the other believed he had found the philosopher's stone using biochemistry and homeopathy, a third saw Count Pückler as the savior of the twentieth century,[128] a fourth had discovered a revolutionary new monetary theory, and a fifth revealed the causal

---

[128] Count Walter von Pückler was a passionately anti-Semitic aristocrat and lawyer from Prussia. He often engaged in fanatical agitation against Jews and made fanciful claims, such as that he was following the direct and personal commands of Jesus Christ himself.

relationship between National Socialism and nuclear fission. They linked all these more or less arcane activities as best they could to the Party and its aspirations. The esotericists confused their grotesque fads with National Socialism and demanded that the Party align itself with their shameless and arrogant demands, lest the Party squander and fritter away its entire historical mission.

Only unwavering firmness can help against this kind of damage. We have never allowed such fantasies to flourish in our movement, and many a *völkisch* world reformer who wandered around in sandals, a backpack, and a hunter's shirt saw himself expelled from the Party without further ado.

*   *   *

The police department clearly did not want to have the question of the ban decided before an ordinary court. Certainly, I was often summoned to Moabit for the matter concerning Stucke, the drunken pastor; however, neither the case, nor it seems the courage, was sufficient among the responsible authorities for a trial.

Nonetheless, the Party was still banned, and all our cries of protests against it had no effect. The national press still refused to support us; in fact, they were probably very happy with the obstacles placed on an annoying competitor in the capital of the Reich, and they believed that maintaining the long-standing bourgeois order and calmness depended on our being outlawed.

Our offices on Lützow Street were then a kind of "headquarters for conspiring." Regular work was becoming more and more impossible. Almost every week, police came to search the building. The street itself was swarming with snitches and provocateurs. Our files and paperwork had been sheltered in the private homes of Party members. We had posted large signs on the door stating that the offices of the National Socialist members of the Reichstag were located here. Of course, this never stopped the police from searching these places at will and hindering our work in every way.

We encountered no resistance, and the enemy was no longer even facing us. Wherever we tried to attack him, he evaded. He had taken refuge behind the tried-and-true tactic of ignoring us, and no political trick could lure him out of his shelter. There was absolutely no more talk about us. National Socialism was taboo in Berlin. The press pointedly avoided even mentioning our names. In the Jewish newspapers, as if by an unspoken order, the articles castigating us disappeared, too. They had ventured too far forward, and they were now trying to make people forget the all-too-shrill howls of the past few months by keeping silent.

For us, this was much more unbearable than a brutal yet open attack, because this meant we were condemned to be totally ineffective. The enemy hid like a coward and sought to annihilate us with silence and contempt.

National Socialism was to be a mere episode in the capital city. They wanted to gradually neutralize it by ignoring it so that they could move on to current affairs by the time fall began.

In Moabit, National Socialist SA men stood before the judges every day. This one had worn the outlawed brown uniform, that one had endangered public order and security by displaying a Party badge, and this other had slapped an insolent and arrogant Jew on the Kurfürstendamm. They were made to pay the penalty for these crimes with heavy, draconian sentences. Six months was the minimum prison sentence to which our SA men were condemned for ridiculous trifles. The press no longer even reported on it. It gradually became a natural fact of life.

We could understand that the Jewish newspapers worked according to a calculated long-term plan. Their goal was to paralyze National Socialism, to bury it without ceremony, to gag its leaders and speakers. But what we could never understand is how the bourgeois press aided and abetted this shameful scheme. At the time, it was possible for them to help the National Socialist movement in Berlin to stay afloat. This was not doing us a favor but simply giving voice to a just cause. They should have demanded that at least the KPD also be banned, since the National Socialist movement was. Even assuming that what we were accused of was really true, the communists had a history much bloodier than ours. But the bourgeois press did not dare to come down on the KPD, because the communists were the political children of social democracy. It was known that wherever they were attacked, all of Judah stood as an ally for each other, and they were facing a united front from Ullstein and Mosse to the Karl Liebknecht House.[129]

---

[129] Leopold Ullstein was a Jewish newspaper proprietor, and Rudolf Mosse was a Jewish publisher of a great deal of newspapers; the two of them were sympathetic to capitalism. The Karl Liebknecht House served as the headquarters for the

At the time, in our despair and in the face of the seemingly inevitable decay of our Berlin organization, we learned to never place any hope whatsoever in the bourgeoisie. The bourgeoisie is cowardly. It is afraid of making decisions and lacks character and courage in its convictions. In the bourgeois press, it is fashionable to howl with the wolves, but none of them is bold enough to speak out against the wolves. It was fashionable to persecute National Socialism. Jewish writers had accused us of mediocrity, and in intellectual circles we were considered unintelligent and uneducated, vulgar and annoying. A decent person would want nothing to do with us. This was the unwritten law for public opinion. The intellectual philistine joined the chorus of persecutors for fear of being considered backward and outdated. Our movement was surrounded on all sides. Sick, tired, and dejected, we followed the inevitable course of events. The Party was slipping out of our hands, and attempts to hoist it up once again with a bold and aggressive paper of our own had failed across the board. It seemed as if it had been decided that we would not have a place in the capital of the Reich.

Back then, we often momentarily lost faith in our future, yet we continued to work—not out of enthusiasm but out of desperate hatred. We did not want to let our adversaries have the satisfaction of bringing us to our knees. In a seemingly irreversible decay, defiance constantly gave us new courage to persevere and keep fighting.

From time to time, fate was kind to us. Our editor-in-chief's prison sentence finally came to an end one day. Exhausted and dejected, he came back from Moabit to silently and resolutely return to his work. *Der Angriff* soon saw its quality improve. Work resumed with renewed strength.

For the first time, a glimmer of light pierced through the dark cloud that hung ominously over us. Already we were beginning to hope again; already we were making new plans. The worries were left behind, as we marched courageously forward. We did not want to surrender. We were firmly convinced that one day fate would not refuse its blessings and its grace to those who remained steadfast through the turmoil, distress, and danger!

German Communist Party (KPD); Karl Liebknecht was a communist revolutionary who was put to death after a failed insurrection.

10. Nuremberg, 1927

Party rallies have always played a special role in the history of the National Socialist movement. They were landmarks in the great evolution of the Party's activism. We took stock of the work accomplished, and we determined, in guiding political resolutions, the tactical line of the future struggle.

The Party rally in 1923 significantly influenced the critical decisions that were made within the movement during that year of turmoil.[130] In November 1923, the Party launched its final assault, and when this failed, the movement as a whole was banned by the authorities throughout Germany.[131] The leaders of the Party ended up incarcerated, while the organization itself was dismantled, the freedom of its press infringed, and its members scattered to the winds.

When Adolf Hitler was released in December 1924, he immediately made arrangements to restore the Party, and in February 1925, the old movement was reborn. At the time, Hitler estimated that five years would suffice to rebuild the movement so that it could intervene decisively in the course of politics; his prediction proved prophetic. These five years were filled with tireless work, militant enthusiasm, and revolutionary mass activism.

Certainly, at the time it was re-established, the movement had to practically start from scratch, and this seemed all the more difficult

---

[130] The NSDAP's very first Party rally was held in Munich in January 1923. Following the Party's ban later that year, there would not be another until July 1926.
[131] This was the year of the thwarted Beer Hall Putsch, in which fifteen Party members were killed by the Bavarian authorities.

as it had for a certain time assumed a level of political importance, and had then suddenly found itself thrown into oblivion. In 1925, we were not yet able to present before a Party rally the results of the new task we had undertaken. The organization was again in its very early stages. In most parts of the country, it worked under police surveillance, and sometimes even under local bans that had not yet been lifted. Our supporters had not yet been brought together into an organic unit. The Party leadership, therefore, had no other choice but to forgo the rally and instead to intensify the Party's activism with all its might.

In 1926, we were firmly re-established. The movement had successfully overcome the preliminary difficulties and had once again created solid points of support, in every *Gau* and in every large city. In the summer of 1926, the first major Party rally since the collapse of 1923 was held in the city of Weimar. This in itself was an unexpected success, given the balance of power at the time. Work immediately resumed with a vengeance. The Party gradually began to break off the shackles of anonymity and burst into the public eye as a decisive political force.

In 1927, it was finally possible to organize a much more impressive Party rally. Nuremberg was chosen as the location, and an appeal was made to the entire movement to be a living testimony to the unbreakable strength and power of the revived Party, in unity and discipline.

Party rallies for the NSDAP are very different from those held by other parties. In keeping with the democratic parliamentary character of their organizers, those are simply intended as an opportunity for cheap discussion. Party representatives from all parts of the country gather there for meetings that are most often Platonic.[132] The Party's political beliefs are subjected to a critical evaluation, and the conclusion of these debates is then expressed each day in pompous exercises of style, in their so-called resolutions. Most often, these resolutions are of no historical value. They are only calculated to appeal to the public. Through them, they often seek to artificially shroud the underlying contradictions that have arisen within their party. No one finds this more embarrassing and painful than those who for a whole year have worked devotedly and unwaveringly in the country for their movement.

---

[132] "Platonic" in this sense means the discussions are confined only to theories and ideals, and do not result in or bring about any practical action.

Most of the time the representatives of these parties leave the conference with a heavy heart. They just became even more acutely aware of the cracks within their movement. Their unproductive debates only become more heated and give the public the pathetic spectacle of members on the same team quarreling and going back and forth with one another. The work done at these party conferences is generally, from a political point of view, equal to nothing. Subsequent party policy is barely influenced by it. The high priests of the party merely provide themselves with an excuse for the coming year with forged expressions of trust. Then they continue the old policy with the old methods in the old format. The resolutions, with their strong and emphatic tone, in reality only serve to keep the party's restless activists at bay under the leadership of the bureaucrats.

Our Party rally is filled with a completely different spirit. It is not simply a get-together for the civil servants and full-time representatives of the Party, but this is a gathering of the entire organization. Every Party member, especially every SA man, considers it a special honor to be personally present at a Party rally, to work among the totality of members who participate. The rally does not result in a barren exchange of words. On the contrary, it must provide the public with a unified image of the Party, one of resolution and an unshakeable fighting spirit; it must visibly demonstrate the inherent connection between the Party's leadership and its base. At the Party rally, our activists gain new courage and new strength. The rhythmic beating of the SA battalions' marching steps galvanizes and fortifies them, as should the vigorous and uncompromising resolutions adopted. From the Party rally, our activists return to their mission feeling reborn.

The Party rally of 1926 in Weimar had given the leaders, the Party members, and the SA men who gathered there this immense reserve of strength, with which they were able to fight through strenuous political battles until August 1927. The impact of this prodigious display of force was felt in our work for over a year. Now, the Party rally of 1927 in Nuremberg had to prove that the Party had not become stagnant or even lost ground since then. On the contrary, it needed to demonstrate that the Party's work was successful throughout the Reich and that the Party could present the irrepressible image of a new political power for the whole of Germany.

The Party rally should express the unity and resolution of the entire movement without falling into an internal quarrel over political

doctrine and tactics, and those parts of the country where the movement had been opposed and terrorized for years are especially entitled to this.

The Party members of Berlin expected more from the Nuremberg rally than a simple gathering of activists. In the past year, they
had to endure the most difficult battles. They had emerged from
these struggles strengthened and seasoned, and now the opportunity
to express the unshakeable resolve of the Berlin organization was offered to them, without the pressure of the authorities or being
gagged.

Preparations for this Party rally took months. The stronger the
pressure from outside became, the more the joy and anticipation
grew as we awaited this mass demonstration. The Berlin Party member and SA man came here to seek new strength for the coming
struggle. They wanted to be carried away by the massive parades for
which the organization of the entire Reich came together, from north
to south, from east to west.

Three weeks before the rally, around fifty unemployed SA men
left Berlin on foot for Nuremberg. As soon as they had stepped beyond the border of the capital, they once again donned their good
old uniform and marched the hundreds of miles that separated them
from their heartfelt desire.

It may be difficult for the bourgeois to believe that, despite the
ban on the Party, we had chartered three trains from Berlin to Nuremberg for this event, hiding this massive exodus from the eyes of
the authorities. And yet it was so.

*   *   *

On the Saturday before the Party rally (which was the prelude to
this great National Socialist event, so to speak), we were already certain that this gathering would be a smash hit for the movement. More
than forty trains from all over the Reich were chartered, and they all
arrived at Nuremberg Central Station in the morning. In addition, an
enormous number of participants flocked to the old imperial city by
foot, bicycle, and truck.

"The National Socialist movement is dead!" Or so our enemies
had gleefully assumed for two years. And then the exact opposite was
true. The movement not only remained intact under the blows of

government persecution, but it had victoriously withstood them and now stood stronger than ever.

The name of Nuremberg alone greatly fascinated most Party members. For them, it was the epitome of Germany. Within the walls of this city, world-renowned cultural works were created. When one spoke of Nuremberg, one spoke of the best German tradition, which showed the path to a future full of promise.

Once already, in difficult times, the sons of Germany had marched into this city by tens of thousands, welcomed and acclaimed by fellow patriots who believed that the new Reich had already been built. What was then so powerful and inspiring during the most critical period of post-war politics collapsed into itself, as it had not yet been fully molded and shaped, with its great heritage being mismanaged in the unfortunate months following the Party's collapse by individuals ill-equipped for the task.[133]

This time, nationalist Germany once again looked toward Nuremberg, where the National Socialist Brownshirts marched by the tens of thousands, demonstrating for a new state against the tribute policy.[134] The faith and hope of hundreds of thousands guided the victorious march of these young activists, who had proven in a fierce two-year struggle that the National Socialist ideal and its political organization could not be intimidated by any means, including terrorism.

The first attempt failed on November 9th, 1923. It had not fulfilled its historic mission and gave way to chaos for the time being. After a period of deep depression, the rebuilding of the movement began in February 1925, and now it was to be shown for the first time that the status of the Party was completely different from that of 1923, that the movement was once again at the forefront of nationalist revolutionary Germany.

Full of faith and confidence, the nation witnessed this parade of the National Socialist masses. Every SA man felt that he was marching alongside his comrade like the sharp tip of a steel sword. It was his boldness, his bravery, and his tenacious perseverance that had led him this far. He moved through these days filled with pride and

---

[133] This is alluding to the time during which Hitler was imprisoned and the National Socialist movement greatly suffered without his leadership.

[134] The "tribute policy" refers to the reparations enforced against Germany by the Allied powers as a punishment for the First World War.

The march from Berlin to Nuremberg

exaltation. He had picked up the fallen flag, carrying it forward through the darkness. The banner was firmly planted. Everywhere, in every city, in every village, the people recognized the shining flag of the National Socialist awakening, and where they did not want to learn to love the movement, they had at least learned to hate and fear it.

They came from factories, from mines and offices, from plows and harrows, and in their midst stood the leader of the movement. We were grateful to him that the policy of the movement had not changed one bit. He guaranteed that it would remain that way in the future.

Today, there was neither author nor laborer, neither farmhand nor civil servant. Today, they were all the remaining Germans who did not want to despair about the future of the nation. They were the bearers of the future, the guarantee that Germany was destined not for failure but for freedom. For hundreds of thousands and millions, they had become the symbol of a new faith. If it were not for them, everyone knew that then Germany would have to despair. Their hearts full of pride and their flags held aloft in the wind, they marched forward, letting the rhythm of their cadenced steps resound vibrantly within the walls of the old imperial city.

A young Germany stood up and demanded its rights. Its flags fluttered over the city; those whose blood had flowed under these flags were countless, and countless were those who had been thrown into prison or who had fallen under them.

They did not want to forget that. Above all, they did not want to forget the day when these flags, under a bright sun and cheered by tens of thousands, were carried through the streets of the city.

Der Angriff published a special issue for the first time on the occasion of the Nuremberg rally. On the front page, an electrifying drawing: a chained fist breaks free from its shackles and flourishes an unfurled flag. Below it, this laconic text:" Banned but not dead!"

This was what every Berlin comrade and SA man subconsciously felt. The movement had victoriously overcome all the crises and all the murderous blows. With daring boldness, it had defied a preposterous and implacable ban, and now it was parading openly to show the public that it could perhaps be banned but never destroyed.

Preliminary deliberations began on Friday afternoon. The participants in the conference sat in specific special groups, which, as such, prefigured the estates general of the future Reich.[135] The sessions were imbued with moral gravity and the deepest sense of

---

[135] This is known as a corporatist arrangement. According to such an arrangement, members of the Reichstag (or "estates general," as Goebbels calls it here) would not represent electoral districts but rather the different trades and industries of Germany—not necessarily specific businesses, but the industries overall. In theory, they would come together to negotiate and agree on public policy in light of their common interests, which would indirectly reflect the interests of the nation. A real-world example of this arrangement was seen with the Chamber of Fasces and Corporations in Fascist Italy.

responsibility. The points up for debate were—and this is not a contradiction—settled almost without debate, as there was unanimity among the delegates on every question. We did not talk, but we acted and made firm resolutions. From these exchanges of views, the official rapporteurs formulated their proposals, which were passed on to the conference at its opening the next day. There were no votes. This would have been rather pointless since they would always have presented the same image of unanimity and resolution.

Outside, the drums were already beating. The chartered trains of Brownshirts began rolling in.

Saturday saw a light drizzle of rain. At dawn, Nuremberg presented a completely new face as soon as one entered the city. Train after train arrived. One after the other, long columns of Brownshirts marched to their quarters across the city. Music was playing in the streets, which were adorned with flags.

The conference opened around noon. The spacious hall was filled with attendees in a jovial mood. A set of doors opened, and to the endless cheers of the spectators, Adolf Hitler entered the room with the Party leaders.

In a series of short, inspiring speeches, the Party's policy was clearly and uncompromisingly defined. The conference continued until seven o'clock in the evening, and Nuremberg was then entirely dominated by the advancing National Socialist movement. Around ten o'clock in the evening, when the endless columns of torch-bearing SA men marched in front of the Führer at the Deutscher Hof,[136] everyone was aware that this party represented a rock in the middle of the raging sea of German collapse.

Finally, it was the big day. Mist still covered the city when the SA men gathered at eight o'clock in the morning for a big roll call at Luitpoldhain.[137] Section by section, the brown detachments moved out with exemplary discipline until, after an hour, the large terraces were filled with tightly packed troops.

When Hitler appeared to his loyal supporters, amid endless cheers, the sun burst out from the dark clouds. The presentation of the new flag began. The old colors have been humiliated; the flag of

---

[136] The Deutscher Hof was a historical hotel in Nuremberg. Hitler often stayed there during his visits to Nuremberg.

[137] Luitpoldhain was a park on the Party rally grounds. It was named after Luitpold, Prince Regent of Bavaria.

the old Reich has been dragged through the dirt. We give to our faith a new symbol.

"Forward, march!" There were thousands and thousands crowding the streets. Flowers, flowers, and more flowers! Each SA man was adorned like a victorious warrior returning to the homeland after a battle.

The parade took place at the main market square in front of an immense crowd that stretched endlessly for hours. A constant stream of Brownshirts marched in and saluted their Führer. The sun shone brightly above us. Again and again, there were flowers as young Germany marched.

The battle-hardened Berlin SA was at the head of the march. They were showered with cheers and flowers. For the first time here, the hearts of the German people answered them.

Mixed in with them were those laborers without labor who, one day in July, set out for Nuremberg from Berlin, their backpacks filled only with literature. Every day, regardless of the weather, they walked fifteen miles, and when they stopped in the evening, they took no time to rest or relax, so that they could spread their political ideals late into the evening.

In some of the big cities, they were met with spitting and beatings, but that would not deter them. They marched on and arrived in Nuremberg ahead of schedule.

Then they marched with their comrades. Seven hundred SA men from the banned Berlin organization found their way to Nuremberg by foot, bicycle, truck, and train. For months, they had eaten less, given up beer and tobacco, and some had even literally starved—all to raise the money for this trip. They lost two days' worth of wages, and the price of the chartered train alone was twenty-five marks. Some of these men earned only twenty marks in a week.

Nonetheless, the SA man was able to save up for the trip, and that Saturday morning, alongside his comrades, he got off the wagons that took them from Berlin to Nuremberg with a pounding heart. In the evening, he marched with tens of thousands of others in front of the Führer, bearing his burning torch proudly and saluting. His eyes were shining. He truly did not know whether any of this was real. At home, he was only insulted, ridiculed, beaten, and thrown into prison. And there, all along the streets, thousands and thousands of people were greeting him and shouting, "Heil!"

Above the old imperial city, the deep blue sky stretched like an immense vault; the air was as clear as glass, and the sun shone brightly, as if it had never seen such a day.

And now the fanfares rung out leading the never-ending columns marching through the street. One would almost believe that such a spectacle could go on forever. On the side, dark walls of people waited for the parade. Not a single cry of protest; on the contrary, they all waved and cheered, as if these were tens of thousands of victorious soldiers, and threw flowers again and again.

Those seven hundred men marched in front. Because they had fought the hardest of battles for a year, they were now showered with flowers. They put them on their belts, ever more numerous. Their hats soon became nothing more than bouquets of blooming flowers, and little girls laughed and waved at them. At home, they were spat upon instead.

And now the parade passed the Führer. By the thousands, by the tens of thousands, they saluted him, shouting," Heil!" We barely heard each other. They took the flowers from their belts and tossed them to the cheering crowd.

"Pass in review!"[138] Their legs flew as the band performed "Parademarsch der langen Kerls."[139]

And then the evening arrived, tiring and heavy. It started to rain. In a captivating final meeting of Party delegates, the concentrated revolutionary force of the movement was once again manifested. The streets outside were filled with jubilant and enthusiastic people. It was as if the new Reich had arisen.

Drum rolls and pipes playing. An enthusiasm brought forth only by the pure heart of German youth full of yearning. In seven mass meetings, the great orators of the Party spoke in the evening to tens of thousands of listeners.

Night now fell upon us. A great blessed day was coming to an end. For all who took part, it must have been a font of strength for an entire year of work, worry, and struggle.

---

[138] The review is a ceremonial inspection of military (in this case, paramilitary) forces typically performed by a commander of some sort, Hitler being the commander here.
[139] This translates to "Parade March of the Tall Men." It is a military march originally composed in 1922 and named after the so-called Potsdam Giants who served in the Old Prussian Sixth Infantry Regiment, from 1675 to 1806.

Do you know that you are persecuting your own brother?

And now, time to tighten the straps on the helmet!

*　　　*　　　*

Late in the evening, the Berlin SA men left the old imperial city on their chartered trains. But as they approached Berlin, a surprise awaited them that no one would expect. The trains were suddenly brought to a halt in Teltow, and the entire station was occupied by police officers and detectives.[140] Out of an abundance of caution, they searched for weapons, and then they conducted the most absurd experiment: seven hundred National Socialists, who had left Berlin for their Nuremberg conference completely peacefully, were arrested on the spot and brought to the Berlin police headquarters in trucks they had prepared beforehand.

For once, it was a true stroke of genius from Alexanderplatz. Back then, it was the first time that a mass arrest had been carried out using this method, and it therefore caused a great stir throughout the country and abroad. With carbines and raised batons aimed at them, seven

---

[140] Teltow is a town approximately eleven miles southwest from the Berlin city center.

hundred innocent men were arrested en masse and brought into police custody.

However, it gets worse. The manner in which they were arrested was much more heinous. It was known that the Führer had solemnly presented the Berlin SA with two new flags. They understood that these two flags had been taken on the train with all the other honored and glorious flags of the Berlin SA, and the police had no shame in seizing these esteemed symbols of the movement's struggle.

At the last moment, a young SA man had a desperate idea. He cut the cloth off his flag and hid it under his brown shirt.

"What do you have there under your shirt? Show us!"

The boy turned pale. A dirty hand ripped open his brown shirt, and then this kid got red-hot. He raged and scratched and spat. It took eight men to subdue him. In the end, his beloved flag was torn from his chest in shreds.

Was this anything the police should be proud of? Does it bring honor to the police of a civilized state?

The boy had tears in his eyes. He stood up suddenly, and standing among his comrades, he began to sing. The one next to him joined in, and then more and more until everyone was singing. It was no longer a transfer of detainees transported in thirty or forty trucks through the streets of Berlin, which was just waking up—it was yet another parade of young heroes.

"Deutschland, Deutschland über alles!" is what the chorus sang throughout the journey in the trucks.[141] The bourgeois rubbed his eyes in astonishment. He had been told that the National Socialist movement was dead. He believed that the ban and the persecution and the prison sentences had dealt us a death blow. And now we stood up vigorously, full of courage, with no obstacle able to hinder our progress.

Seven hundred men were crammed together as prisoners in a large hall. They were called one by one before an interrogator. They introduced themselves to him defiantly and boldly and with stereotypical indifference answered each question unwaveringly with, "I refuse to give any information." All this was accompanied by our comrades singing, "Freedom is not yet lost!"

---

[141] "Deutschland, Deutschland über alles!" is a line from the national anthem of Germany at the time.

To whom God gives power . . .

These SA men could march against the devil. They had planted their outlawed flags in their hearts. There they were safe, and the day was not far off when they would rise again in shining purity. It was of course necessary to quickly release the seven hundred apprehended men without any further action. They had committed no crime, but it was not about that at all.

The police only wanted to once again display their arbitrary power to their defeated opponent. They wanted to demonstrate that they were on guard. The next day, when the seven hundred men returned to work, more than one found his place taken by someone else.

The laborer returned to his machine and saw that he had already been replaced by a colleague. One is easily thrown into the street in this democracy of freedom and fraternity! The clerk returned to his office and found a notice of a disciplinary action on his desk. He was finally guaranteed the freedom of opinion when the reactionaries were defeated and the freest state in the world was founded!

As we later learned, the Berlin police operation in Teltow, which consisted of the seemingly senseless arrest of seven hundred National Socialists returning from the Nuremberg rally, proved to be not unsuccessful for those who had perpetrated it. According to Party estimates, seventy-four employed men among those arrested, who had lost a day of work owing to police interrogations, were fired and lost their jobs and their livelihoods. Among those who had been subject to administrative reprimands, there were a whole host of senior, middle, and junior civil servants, accountants, and stenographers, and a majority of the victims were craftsmen from the most diverse professional occupations.

With such a feat, they were certainly proud. They must have had the satisfying feeling of having harmed people who could not be prosecuted under the provisions of the law, by inflicting financial and professional injury on them. After all, it was revenge, petty but effective.

Der Angriff responded in its own way. In its next issue, it published a caricature depicting Dr. Bernhard Weiss, Berlin's deputy police chief, in an inimitably grotesque situation. He stood there, a pair of large-framed glasses on his big nose, his hands clasped behind his back, looking in astonishment at an SA man who, with his brown, flower-adorned hat, approached him with a wide grin, holding out a Nuremberg funnel.[142] The caption read, "To whom God gives power. . . ."[143] And below, "We brought back a small gift from Nuremberg for dear Bernhard."

But this is what the administration wrote:

Berlin, August 30th, 1927
The Chief of Police
Entry No. 1217 P 2-27
Dear Detective Kurt Krischer, Department IV:
   Owing to your participation in the Nuremberg trip of the banned Berlin organization of the National Socialist German Workers' Party in so-called Hitler uniform and the fact that several copies of the newspaper *Der Angriff* and Party membership forms were found in your possession, I conclude that you continue to campaign for a banned organization. This activity is incompatible with your position as a public servant.

---

[142] "Nuremberg funnel" is the literal translation of a German figure of speech that refers to a forceful manner of teaching a concept. Here, it implies Weiss is using a heavy-handed approach to "teach" the National Socialists a different ideology.
[143] The full proverb, translated from German, is, "To whom God gives power, he also gives intelligence." It is usually understood to mean that even incompetent statements by those in power are meaningful and authoritative. In the cartoon, it is a sarcastic display of subservience to Weiss.

Therefore, I am obliged to notify you without delay of your termination of service as of the thirty-first of this month.

Signed, Zörgiebel

This was the goal, and that was the method. Worry and distress once again fell upon the movement. Many of its members paid for their participation in the Nuremberg rally with hunger, poverty, and unemployment. However, this also had its upside. In the ranks of the Party members, anger and indignation reached its boiling point. But this time, they did not give vent to their anger with senseless acts of violence. Rather, they focused on work and success. The great enthusiasm that had run through the National Socialist mass demonstration in Nuremberg was carried over into the gloomy worries of everyday life. What could the ban on speaking, the financial difficulties, and the dissolution of the Party do to us now? The Berlin organization had shown the entire movement that it could withstand the shock and that we all must remain on our guard anywhere in the Reich; it had also proven that we were not fighting alone, but that on the contrary our struggle was reverberating throughout the National Socialist movement. The entire Party stood behind the Berlin organization and ardently supported the furtherance of the struggle.

The Party rally began to work its effects on our daily duties. The off-season was over; summer with all its worries and miseries was behind us. Rigid political life was beginning to thaw. With new strength, we marched toward new goals. And above all, the days of Nuremberg shone like a beacon leading us to victory!

11. Overcoming the Crisis

Here are some samples of administrative correspondence following the Nuremberg rally:

Police Headquarters—Section 1A
Dear Reichstag Representative Dietrich-Franken:
Regarding the complaint that you transmitted to me personally yesterday, I inform you that I have no objection to the return of the confiscated badges currently in the possession of the treasurer of the Office of Representatives.
I am also prepared to have the confiscated flags returned, if it can be established beyond doubt that they belong to non-local chapters of the NSDAP.
The Chief of Police
p.p. Wündisch

Police Headquarters—Section 1A
Subject: Letter dated August 25th, 1927, concerning the ban on Dr. Goebbels
Dear Mr. Heinz Haake:
Owing to the dissolution of the NSDAP in Greater Berlin, any activity by the dissolved organization within this district is unacceptable. The only exception to this is public meetings in which NSDAP members of the Reichstag alone act as speakers in favor of the views of the party they represent, insofar as it concerns elections. An appearance by the former leader of

the Berlin NSDAP, Dr. Goebbels, as a speaker at election meetings of the NSDAP in Berlin cannot therefore be permitted, as this would be seen as a resumption of NSDAP activity in Greater Berlin. Should Dr. Goebbels nonetheless appear as a speaker at meetings of the NSDAP, I shall immediately disperse said meetings.

p.p. and notarized: Krause, Secretary of Chancery

The response from *Der Angriff*:

I, Krause, will therefore punch the constitution in the face, deny Dr. Goebbels the freedom guaranteed to every German to express his opinion, and if he still dares to open his mouth, disperse the meeting.

Cruel Krause, we learn with trembling of your terrible threats. We will therefore not fail to ask before every meeting, very timidly: "Is Krause around?"

But first, we take our diaries in hand to write down your name.

A caricature from *Der Angriff*: A small Jew, who is easily recognized as the deputy chief of police of Berlin, Dr. Weiss, sits on a box, with his head hung in worry. He keeps the lid of this box closed with all his might. On the box it is written," NSDAP Berlin."

The image next to it: A smiling SA man bursts out of the box, causing the Jew to fly high into the air. It is captioned," Right when you think you've got it, it jumps out of the box."

An SA man found himself in dire straits following his arrest in Teltow. He was one of those laid off from work as a result. But his boss did not believe that an unlawful arrest was the reason for his absence from work. The SA man in question wrote to the chief of police and requested a written confirmation of the reasons which led to his arrest in Teltow, so that he could provide his boss with it. Here was the response:

Police Headquarters—Section 1A
Dear Mr. J. Schmidt of Berlin:
 I am unable to fulfill your request of August 24th, 1927, to produce an official written confirmation of the reasons for your arrest on Monday, August 22nd, 1927, at Teltow station.
Signed Wündisch

Here is how it goes with bans:

Right when you think you've got it . . .

. . . it jumps out of the box!

Deutsche Volksgenossen

Heraus zur großen öffentlichen Wählerversammlung am Freitag, den 23. September 1927, abends 8 Uhr, in der Schloßbrauerei Schöneberg, Hauptstraße 122, 123.

Es spricht der nationalsozialistische Landtagsabgeordnete Heinz Haake über das Thema:

Deutschenverfolgung in Berlin!

Freie Aussprache! Saalöffnung 7¹⁄₂ Uhr. Unkostenbeitrag 30 Pfg. Erwerbslose 10 Pfg.

Lest und abonniert den „Völkischen Beobachter". Herausgeber Adolf Hitler.

Poster for the "bloody brawl" in Schöneberg: "Representative Heinz Haake will speak about the persecution of Germans in Berlin!"

From an article in *Der Angriff* on Monday, September 26th, 1927:

They arrest people senselessly. Anyone who utters a single remark about police brutality is arrested. A harmless citizen, who is just passing by, receives a blow to the lower back with a rifle butt. Stunned, he turns around, and a brute in a green uniform shouts in his face, "Keep it moving, or I'll kick your head in!"

When Dietrich, a member of the Reichstag, went to the police station to visit the arrestees, he was physically assaulted there. A severely disabled veteran accompanying him was thrown to the ground when he dared to speak up for a woman whose blouse had been torn open after a police officer named Laube made the most vile comment.

From the same issue:

A bloody brawl in Schöneberg. Following an election meeting of *Landtag* Representative Haake, violent clashes with the communists broke out. As one of the three communist speakers could not present a party membership card, he was not authorized to speak, in compliance with the order of the police. Most of the participants having already left the room, the numerous communists present after the meeting ended then used beer mugs and chair legs to attack the other attendees, including Dr. Goebbels and Representative Haake. During the fight, the communists were chased from the room with their injuries and fled every which way. Subsequently, National Socialists returning home were individually attacked. The police department bears responsibility for the ban and the subsequent attacks.

From the same issue:

> A heinous attack. As Dr. Goebbels' chauffeur, Albert Tonak, was returning home from the meeting on Friday, red thugs ambushed him right outside his house. He was critically injured with two stab wounds to the arm and another to the stomach.

*   *   *

September 10th, 1927
Berlin Police Union
Dear Detective Kurt Krischer of Berlin:
   At the meeting on the sixth of this month, the Berlin Police Union has reviewed your letter of dismissal and unanimously concluded that you bear responsibility for your dismissal. It is, therefore, unable to accept your objection or represent you in a possible lawsuit.

On behalf of K. Meyer,
Secretary

On Monday, October 2nd, 1927, Field Marshal Paul von Hindenburg celebrated his eightieth birthday. The nationalist Femerichter, who had defended the honor and reliability of the German army in the most difficult times with all their strength and dedication, sometimes until their dying breath, remained imprisoned in penal servitude.[144]

---

[144] The Femerichter were certain members of the so-called Black Reichswehr, a private paramilitary organization that was used to supplement the Weimar Republic's armed forces in an attempt to circumvent the Versailles Treaty. The Femerichter would allegedly assassinate leftist politicians and other "enemies of the Reich," as well as Black Reichswehr servicemen who were suspected of betraying the organization. Several members of the Black Reichswehr were arrested in connection with one of these murders and condemned to death in March 1927. Paul von Hindenburg, as President of Germany, would eventually commute their sentences in

Albert Tonak, Dr. Goebbels' chauffeur since 1926, was critically injured five times in the struggle for Berlin, the first time at the Pharus Hall.

An article in *Die Rote Fahne* toward the end of September 1927:

The Chief Bandit Resurfaces.

The response from *Der Angriff:*

First of all, Dr. Goebbels, the so-called chief bandit, does not need to resurface, because he had never been in hiding. Rather, he dared, despite the ban that weighs on him, to open his mouth several times at the tumultuous meeting in Schöneberg to call for peace and to put an end to the emerging disorder.

Without his calls for peace, the storm would have broken out much sooner given the provocative attitude of the Bolshevik shock troops, and the meeting would not have lasted until the end. . . .

It was not exactly a feat for the communist horde to remain in the hall and wait until only a small group of National Socialist voters remained with Dr. Goebbels and Representative Haake, to then attack this group. Far from a feat, because

February 1928 to life imprisonment. Ultimately, they were released in October 1930 in an act of political amnesty.

these cowards know full well that we cannot, under the ban, organize our security service as usual.

Despite everything, this cowardly attack with beer mugs, chair legs, and coffee cups went poorly for them, because the National Socialists, with their leaders at the forefront, defended themselves. And in the blink of an eye, all the low-life scum were thrown out of the room. But their leader, a sort of scruffy criminal who, while the meeting was still going on, had sought to cause an uproar with his incessant disruptive heckling, had hidden from the start of the fight in . . . the ladies' room.

The police department undoubtedly bears real responsibility for the entire incident, following the unconstitutional and unwarranted ban on the Berlin organization. If the Jewish press, from the *Berliner Tageblatt* to *Die Rote Fahne*, became angry that we only allowed debate opponents who can present membership cards from the opposite camp into our meeting and if that caused disorder during the meeting, then these gentlemen, as the chairman of the meeting had already noted, ought to complain to the responsible authority, that is, the police department that has introduced such a procedure, under penalty of a fine of one thousand Reichsmark in the event of an infraction.

I was to receive the following letter:

Berlin, September 29th, 1927
Entry No. 2083 1A 1-27
Dear Dr. Joseph Goebbels of Berlin:
     Your appearance at the last public electoral meeting of the NSDAP in Berlin shows that, despite my order of dissolution dated May 5th, 1927, you are active as a public speaker promoting this dissolved group.
     According to a message I received, Representative Heinrich Haake, member of the *Landtag*, organized and made arrangements for a large public electoral meeting on September 30th, 1927, at eight o'clock in the evening, in the Schwarz banquet hall in Berlin-Lichtenberg. I informed Representative Haake that I only considered this meeting an electoral meeting if NSDAP Representatives alone appear as speakers to present

the ideas of the party they speak for with a view to the next elections. Additionally, only those participants who can be verified as not belonging to the NSDAP are allowed to speak in the debate.

I expressly draw your attention to the fact that you are not authorized to speak at the major public electoral meeting on September 30th, 1927. You are prohibited from speaking before and after the meeting, and also from speaking from your seat or heckling. In the event of an infraction, you are liable, under the dissolution order of May 5th, 1927, to a fine of 1,000 Reichsmark, or in the event of non-payment, to six weeks in prison, in accordance with § 10-217 of the General State Laws of 1796 and § 132 of the Provincial Administration Law of July 3rd, 1883.

p.p. Wündisch
Notarized: Laetermann, Secretary of Chancery

In response to an inquiry from *Landtag* Representative Haake regarding the ban on speaking against Dr. Goebbels in Berlin, the Prussian Ministry of the Interior stated, "Dr. Goebbels is not banned from speaking in Berlin. However, it must be ensured that Dr. Goebbels does not abuse the NSDAP electoral meetings to circumvent the ban on the Berlin group of this party."

A few weeks earlier, one of our friends sent the following letter to a major bourgeois paper:

August 25th, 1927
To whom it may concern at *Berliner Lokal-Anzeiger*:

I have been a reader of the *Berliner Lokal-Anzeiger* for a long time and would therefore like to ask for information on a few points. I have been a reader as I feel the need to read a major national newspaper that wholeheartedly supports the German Reich. I am all the more surprised that for some time you have been publishing misleading articles about the NSDAP. I understand it all the less since the NSDAP is also a pro-German movement whose main purpose is the unconditional fight against Marxism, which you also vigorously oppose in your paper.

A caricature from the same issue of Der Angriff:

Did the man get hit by a car? No, just the Berlin police!

At the NSDAP national conference in Nuremberg, we saw that it was precisely the readers of your newspaper who cheered us on and showered us with flowers. Why do you not even hint at the scale of this massive demonstration of nationalist Germany against Marxism? You report there were about twelve thousand participants. If you had been there, you would know that there were at least five times as many. I advise you to read the official report from the German National Railway. You might then change your opinion.

This was the newspaper's response:

September 9th, 1927
Dear Sir:
According to the very detailed response that we have received in the meantime from our correspondent in Nuremberg, we are obliged to inform you that there is no need for a correction except for a few minor details.
Respectfully yours,

Dr. Breslauer
Berliner Lokal-Anzeiger, Editorial Department

Dr. Breslauer, editor-in-chief of the *Berliner Lokal-Anzeiger*, is a so-called Jewish-German nationalist.

*   *   *

The above documents are only a few sequences from the film that could be called *Battle for Berlin*. These are not earth-shattering events but trifles and trivial matters which, observed in isolation and out of context, do not mean much. However, if we place them in the time and system in which they were possible, they provide a striking and unequivocal image of what the National Socialist movement had to tolerate and endure in Berlin under the ban.

The harassment against us had been so refined that in the end it lost all its effect, and no longer even fomented hatred or indignation, but only cynicism and laughter. It was carried out to the point of absurdity and was so overworked that in the end every blow aimed at us was just a punch in the air.

Ultimately, what is the point of banning someone from speaking if it only confirms the suspicions of a growing number of sympathizers that it is because he speaks the truth? What use is it when we can find more than a hundred ways to circumvent this ban? For example, we might establish a "school of politics" that nominally has nothing to do with our party. The man who has been forbidden to speak is hired there as a professor, and soon it enjoys an audience like no public political meeting in Berlin has seen before.

In this way, the authorities are gradually held up as an object of ridicule. The people lose all respect for them. They lack the size and brutality for a bloodthirsty and ruthless persecution. The persecuted, however, only react to the passive-aggressive politics with smiling contempt. Thus, there is always an antidote to every poison.

Only when an oppressive regime spreads terror, fear, and panic around itself can it end up stunting a movement for a while. However, if it only uses petty harassment, it will always end with the opposite of the desired goal.

The ban no longer stifled us as much, now that we had gotten used to it. The Party responded with indifferent disdain. We were forbidden to gather the activists in Berlin, so we met in Potsdam.

Certainly, there were a few dozen fewer people, but those who came were faithful to the flag, and expressed by their very arrival that they remained devoted to the great cause and persevered in the face of danger. In Potsdam, they proudly and boldly wore their old uniform in the open, parading in brown shirts and hats, with strapped belts and the Party badge pinned to their chests.

On the outskirts of Berlin, they had to put on their civilian clothes again, and there was always a great deal of tomfoolery when they sneaked into the Reich's capital as if into enemy territory. Every time, it was the authorities who were being fooled; they could certainly make things difficult for the movement and its supporters, but had to proceed so convolutedly and so timidly that their victims felt more pleasure than pain.

At the time, the Communist Party believed the moment had come to drown the last remnants of the National Socialist movement in a pool of their own blood. They attacked our activists and speakers in meeting halls in the north and east of Berlin and tried to silence them with force. But for all SA men and Party members, this was just one more reason to come to the next meeting in full force to make these shameless provocations impossible, once and for all. The police department banned the leader of the outlawed movement from intervening during a meeting, including even speaking from his seat. This revealed a fear so petty and childish that the activists felt even more contempt for it.

Since we were forbidden to speak and promote ourselves in Berlin, we went to the surrounding countryside. Around the capital, in the suburbs and villages of Brandenburg, we gathered our comrades, we established solid support points everywhere, and we surrounded the capital of the Reich with a ring of National Socialist bastions. Later, we were able to advance from them into the capital, when the movement was permitted again. We thus conquered firm positions in Teltow and Falkensee, and step by step, we regained ground from the communists during occasionally violent clashes.[145] We embedded ourselves in Brandenburg and intensified the activism there to such an extent that its effects were felt as far as Berlin.

Even in Berlin, we still had the opportunity here and there to engage in activism and public rhetoric. Sometimes news about an event spread among the Party members like wildfire. "Tonight, everyone is

---

[145] Falkensee is a town approximately twelve miles west from the Berlin city center.

going to be at the meeting of this or that party. We are the opposition in the debate." One of us asked to speak, and because we made up the majority of those present, we gave ourselves two or three hours of time to speak, during which we had the opportunity to say what we wanted.

Little by little, the ban lost its effectiveness. In the meantime, *Der Angriff* had transformed. The entire revolutionary power of the Party had been stimulated by the mass momentum of the Nuremberg rally. The crisis of the summer months was gradually overcome, and the hopes of our adversaries were never fulfilled. We dug countermines to destroy their mines, [146] and the persecution organized against us was ultimately doomed to failure.

Financial worries continued to overwhelm us. *Der Angriff* lurched from one financial crisis to another. We had to budget for our newspaper frugally, and only on good days could we pay part of the printer's bills in small installments. But on the other hand, increasing success with our activism brought us income. More and more, the public took notice of our existence. We could no longer be dismissed and ignored. The movement was spreading inexorably and had broken the silent boycott with which people tried to stifle it. We were once again the subject of discussion. Public opinion, to the extent that it retained its last shred of decency, was forced to take our side, and the protest against the petty methods of police repression became more and more vociferous. The extent of expenditures far outweighed the goal sought by Alexanderplatz; they were shooting sparrows with cannons.

The people have an innate sense of justice. If we had collapsed under the ban, no one would have said a word. But as we had overcome it with the last reserves of our own strength, we acquired the sympathies of the broad masses once again. Even the communist himself, deep in his heart, had an ounce of understanding and respect for us. He had to admit that the movement was stronger than his press would have him believe. The Party had barely recovered before the very eyes of the public when it once again enjoyed the respect and favor that the common man is always inclined to show to someone who knows how to impose himself with his own strength despite persecution and repression.

---

[146] Mines and countermines are an element of tunnel warfare. An attacker might dig a mine or tunnel as part of his offense, and the countermine would be dug to destroy the enemy's tunnel and prevent the attack.

The scheme to silence us with administrative restrictions had failed. A frenzied and outrageous press campaign served only to make us better known. The spokesmen of the Party had a name, and the Party itself earned its place on the political scene. We had brought our adversaries out of anonymity, but they, unwittingly, had returned the favor.

The battlefields were demarcated, and the fight continued on. No one could tell us anymore that National Socialism had disappeared from political life in the capital of the Reich. Although banned, the movement had gained new life, the crisis had been overcome victoriously, and the Party was now rushing forward to strike devastating blows!

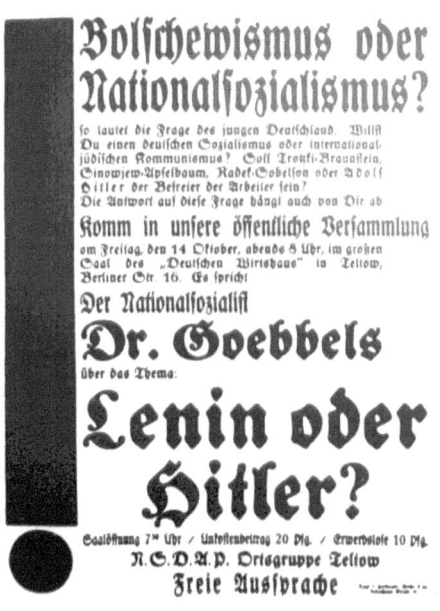

Advertisements were put up all over Berlin. / "Bolshevism or National Socialism?" / "Dr. Goebbels answers the question: Lenin or Hitler?"

12. Banned but Not Dead!

We now had spiritually surmounted the grave organizational crisis into which Berlin's National Socialist movement was thrown by the police ban of May 5th, 1927. The upheaval that had caused severe stress to the Party's structure had been resolved, the break in contact between leadership and the rank and file had been restored thanks to a radical and aggressive weekly newspaper, and the opportunities for activism that we had completely missed during the summer months were recreated. Admittedly, we still had plenty of worries, especially related to finances. But every now and then a streak of light glimmered through the dark clouds that hung over us. And we wanted nothing more in the end than a little hope here and there that we could cling to.

Fate had dealt us a bad hand, and we often had cause to despair and silently abandon our struggle. The new journey of the movement had been interrupted by official action in the Reich's capital, in the midst of the most promising beginnings, and it seemed quite impossible to continue with it, even in a disguised or furtive manner.

Then came the life-saving intervention of *Der Angriff*. It consolidated the Party again. In its columns we had the opportunity to continue to propagate National Socialist ideas in the Reich's capital.

We produced the young enterprise out of thin air, so to speak. It once again proved very clearly that when courage and self-confidence, and also a fair bit of daring, are the inspiration, even the most desperate feats can be achieved. All that is necessary is that those supporting it have faith in their own cause and do not allow the first

195

serious setbacks to force them off the course they once recognized as just.

A great individual once said of himself, "Three things have brought me to the height of my life: a little intelligence, a lot of courage, and a total contempt for money."

We acted on these words. One could not deny some intelligence in the leadership of the National Socialist movement in Berlin. The SA had shown a lot of courage in the difficult battles that were fought night after night for months for the proletarian districts. And a total contempt for money seemed all the more appropriate to us, given that money was in short supply constantly, and this same total contempt is the only way we could remain unperturbed by its scarcity.

Der Angriff faced a serious personnel crisis in the first few months of its existence. The staff who had initially been enthusiastic supporters of the journalistic project flagrantly abandoned our cause when it seemed to become dangerous and hopeless, precipitating our young operation into serious and nearly insurmountable difficulties. For a while we were completely bereft of capable contributors and could only get by with having each political leader agree to write a piece of the newspaper. Thus, most of our time was completely taken up by journalistic work for weeks on end. We published our articles about the struggle under a wide variety of pen names. Nevertheless, although the contributors remained the same, the newspaper had many diverse faces even in this presentation, and the readership had no idea how much care and effort went into writing every single page.

But we were also pleased to see that *Der Angriff* enjoyed ever-increasing importance and respect in the journalism scene of the Reich's capital. It developed differently from the large capitalist newspaper conglomerates. We had no financial backers to provide us with the money we needed to found a newspaper. Then it would be easy to hire an editorial board and publishing staff, and a company could hardly fail. But the inevitable fact is that any newspaper financed by large investors is also obliged to obsequiously represent the political opinion of those behind it. This is not the way to raise a new voice in the chorus of public opinion. A major financier only buys a newspaper of his own so that he may be able to influence public opinion in his favor.

It was the opposite with us. We said what we meant, and since we were not dependent on any financial backing, we were able to express ourselves without holding anything back. By this time we were perhaps the only paper in Berlin that was written out of basic conviction and whose political alignment was not influenced by any undisclosed sources of income. The readers could see this for themselves. Even though the Jewish periodicals, which promoted their own interests, had millions of copies and the general public as readers, their subscribers usually could not relate to them. Nobody is fond of a newspaper like this. The reader only sees them as a necessary evil. He reads them for everyday information. But in the end, he really is convinced that, even if he does not realize it, he is being misled and deceived.

The blind faith in the printed word, which has had such a disastrous effect on public life in Germany, is gradually waning. Today, more than ever, readership demands conviction and sincerity in the opinions from its newspaper.

Since 1918, the masses have become increasingly perceptive and far-sighted. With the industrial revolt that ended the Great War, the international yellow press, as the pacemaker for industrial capitalism, pulled off its last great coup.[147] Since then, industrial capitalism has been on the decline, imperceptibly at first, then at an accelerating pace. The liberal-democratic worldview has long since been intellectually outdated. It now only survives through protocol and parliamentary tricks.

For the masses this means immense disillusionment. We foresaw this disillusionment and very early on built an embankment to channel it. With modern means and an absolutely new and rousing style, we sought to influence public opinion. Of course, our beginnings were primitive and inexpert. But show us a master who was formed in a single day. We, too, had to pay as an apprentice, but we learned something in return. If at present the only way to restrain the National Socialist press is through official bans, then that constitutes classic proof that our journalism is equal to the demands of the times, and that one cannot oppose the views that are expressed by it with intellectual arguments, but only with brute force.

---

[147] This "industrial revolt," of which Goebbels speaks, is colloquially known as "the stab in the back" in English. It refers to the betrayal Germany suffered at the end of the First World War, owing to a number of internal affairs leading to its defeat. The "stab" is the result of Jews, Marxists, and cultural Bolsheviks purposely sabotaging the war effort by fomenting labor strikes and class conflict in an attempt to gain political power. They eventually succeeded in doing so with the establishment of the Weimar Republic by the same republican politicians who had overthrown the German Empire during the 1918 revolution.

Admittedly, we had very few representatives in the Reichstag and the *Landtag*. Nevertheless, the outlawed movement had a way out. The *Gau* office had been converted into an office for parliamentarians. Where Party officials had once worked now resided untouchable representatives of the people. It was not easy to adapt all our habits to this new system. But over the course of the months we got used to it. Gradually, the entire Party organization was brought into line with an illegal state of affairs, so to speak. For our office we developed a new technique that was almost impossible to control. The most important files were dispersed throughout the city in the homes of reliable Party members, and a file was kept only for the Party's Old Guard.

Those who are said to be dead live long!

They stood ready for any emergency. They were armored against any doubt arising from fickleness. So solid and steady, one could build a house on them.

We soon realized that the ban would not be lifted anytime soon. On account of this, we set about reorganizing the entire Party to work around the ban. The former departments became innocuous clubs, although they were often dissolved by the authorities. But a few days later, a disbanded bowling club was transformed into a new club for card games, and the banned swimming club became a conservation society or a soccer team. National Socialism was always present. Despite the ban, the Party's footholds were perfectly intact. The police department felt it was wrong to impose harsh penalties on us, which would have had no legal basis whatsoever. Little by little, new life blossomed from the rubble of the fallen organization.

Not for a moment had the SA tottered. Admittedly its numbers were small, yet well-disciplined, and united into dependable cadres. The few fragile elements that had been with us during the first months of the struggle were gradually expelled. Overall, the core team remained unscathed. By then, almost all the Party members and SA men knew each other personally. The determined faces that we saw week after week, sometimes night after night, at the Party's major events left an indelible mark on our memories. The whole Party was like a big family, and there was a strong sense of belonging to the same community. These were the best days of the Party guard, and it is thanks to them that National Socialism did not disappear from Berlin.

We also took steps to ensure that the nervousness artificially propagated within the Party by outsiders would not threaten the internal well-being of the organization. Attempts at provocation were usually recognized early on and ruthlessly nipped in the bud, as the core of the Party had to be kept intact. This is why, once the ban was lifted, it was easy to rebuild the entire organization.

Our main concern was to provide the Party with tasks and objectives to keep its members busy. By doing so, we prevented the lack of daily activity within the groups from threatening the steady progress of our work with squabbles and manufactured crises.

The ring of well-organized bases that we built around Berlin had soon become a solid chain. We had linked together the immediate environs of the Reich's capital into a large offensive front; this allowed us to retreat to the provinces at any time if the situation in Berlin became too hot.

*   *   *

Every great worldview, if it appears with the bold will to provide the spiritual, cultural, and ultimately material foundations of a people's existence, will have to go through four stages in its development. Whether it is truly chosen by fate will depend on how it manages to bend the forces opposing it during these four stages. A great many ideals have appeared throughout human history. Some men put themselves in the public spotlight claiming that these ideals have meaning to the people and are able to communicate it to them. Thus they come; thus they go. But posterity takes no notice of them. Only few individuals are called upon to give new ideals to the people, and then fate is gracious enough to force these individuals early on to prove to the public that they are not only called but are chosen.

Four critical stages

Every great movement begins in anonymity. It begins with an ideal that springs from the mind of a single person. It is not as if this individual were the inspired inventor of this idea. He alone is blessed by fate to express what the people vaguely feel and longingly sense. He gives expression to the misunderstood desire of the broad masses. We experienced that ourselves when our ideal had grown. It is then usually the case that the common man says, "This is what I have always believed, thought, and valued. It is what I seek, what I feel, and what I surmise."

Only one is chosen, and he now gives expression to the wistful longing and premonitions of the broad masses. Then an organization begins to emerge from the ideal. For the individual who gives the ideal its expression will inevitably strive to win others over, to ensure that he is not left alone, to rally a group, a party, an organization behind him. The organization thus becomes a servant of the ideal.

Of course, his contemporaries will not be able to understand him at first, as he is ahead of his time by a few years or decades. What he absurdly predicts today will become commonplace in twenty years or more. He shows the way to his people; he wants to lead his fellow men from lowly vales to lofty heights. It is to be expected that the present is unwilling, and ultimately unable, to understand him. The first group of supporters of the new ideal remains anonymous for the time being. And that is just as well, because the little oak shoot that so timidly and bashfully breaks through the loose soil for the first time could be snapped and trampled on by a single careless step. It does not yet have the strength to withstand such force. The strength resides only in its roots; that is to say, it only lies in the possibilities of the plant, not in what the plant currently possesses. Of course, it is smaller, more unassuming, and less remarkable than the thicket of weeds, yet that is no indication that it will still be so in ten years' time. After ten years, when that dense growth of weeds has long since been decomposed, a magnificent oak will spread the shadow of its heavy branches all around it.

One does not take notice of this little oak tree at first. Fate, in its wisdom, gives it the opportunity to become what it should be. Nature always ensures that creatures, people, and organizations are only subjected to trials they can overcome.

For the first proponents of a new ideal, the lack of interest from their fellow men is obviously an almost unbearable state. Those who carry within them a combative conviction love to confront the enemy and are happy to grab hold of him and fight. But if the other person does not even see him, does not even notice him, this offensive disdain is the most unbearable thing that can happen to a heroic personality.

Those pioneering champions for a young ideal are, of course, exactly the same in the early stages of the movement as they will be later when they have conquered power, because they themselves do not change; instead, they change those around them. It is not Hitler who has changed, but the Germany in which he lives that has changed.

Fate now examines in this first phase of development whether this man who has appeared with the bold ambition of making history is also strong enough to silently endure anonymity for a while. If he overcomes it without suffering any injury to his soul, fate will consider him ready for the second ordeal. This is because, after a while, the movement will find the inner strength to melt the icy block of spiritual boycott that confines it. It then finds ways and means to make itself known to the public, if not in love, then in hate. If they do not love me, then let them fear me, but at least they will know me. Then soon comes the moment when the public is forced to take notice of the ideal and the organization. One can no longer simply keep silent anymore. When the public is discussing it, when it becomes well-known, then the cowardly newspapers can no longer remain in their dignified silence. Then they have to take a stand, one way or another.

They do so in their own way, because they are convinced that the practices customary at their political level can also be used unconditionally and without any modification in relation to the new movement. However, they are obviously making a fundamental mistake here, because the young movement is founded on an entirely different political principle, is driven by entirely different intellectual motives, has an entirely different style, and represents an entirely different model. It cannot be defeated by the usual, fashionable methods used by its collective opponents. The enemy must realize, to his horror, that everything he thought would harm and put an end to the movement only strengthens and consolidates it. Yes, it just so happens that the very force one uses to oppose the movement is absorbed into the movement itself. At first, they thought they could ridicule it. They put it on the same level as any childish and naive attempt at religion or culture. We old National Socialists still remember exactly the time when we were put on the same footing as the Salvation Army, [148] where general opinion said of us, "They are decent enough, and they are not breaking any laws. They are harmless fools who are best left to themselves."

This is the second phase of development: we are no longer insulted, but we are laughed at. And it is good to be laughed at. If the enemy were to fight us now, he still might be able to stifle the movement. But while he laughs and stands idly by, the movement grows and grows, building strength, breadth, and passion. Yes, the champions of an ideal only feel stronger when their opponents laugh at them. It comes from ambition. Everyone is driven by this ardent desire: "We will wipe those smirks off your face!" The opponent's derisive arrogance only whets the appetite of the supporters of the young movement. They will not abandon their ideal because they are

---

[148] The Salvation Army is a Protestant denomination and an international charitable organization structured in a quasi-military fashion, originally founded to help the poor of London.

being laughed at, but they will make sure that their opponents stop laughing.

That is the second stage. And when the laughter stops, they finally start fighting the movement, first with lies and slander. The opponent has no other choice, because he cannot come up with any better arguments against a new worldview. For example, what ideals could a bourgeois party use to counter the National Socialist movement? How could the Social Democrats stand up to us ideologically?

And they know it. As soon as we take to the podium in an objective political debate, we are the young and they are the old. That is why they try to avoid the fight as much as possible or engage in it with lies and terror. And so, an ocean of filth and slime now pours down on the movement and its leaders. Nothing is too vulgar to sully its reputation. Every day, the enemy fabricates a new horror story. He wallows in his lies. Of course, this will initially make an impression on a crowd of imbeciles devoid of judgment, but only as long as the adversaries can prevent the masses from coming into direct, personal contact with the movement and its leaders. When this is no longer possible, then the enemy is lost; the moment the deceived and fooled masses have the opportunity to get to know the movement and its leaders, they realize the difference between what they were told and what the movement actually stands for. Then the masses feel insulted. The people hate nothing more than being deceived. At first, they come to our meetings with reservations and moral qualms, and then they have to be persuaded that the contradiction between lies and reality is so obvious that the lie crashes down on the liar.

Thus, in the third phase of development, slander quickly becomes persecution. The movement is subjected to the terror tactics of the authorities and the streets. They try to do with violence what they could not do with slander. However, the tragedy of the system is that it always employs its resources too late. Had it done this earlier, it might well have succeeded. But the men who, in the midst of anonymous slander, have rallied behind the movement's flags are no cowards; otherwise, they would not have been able to endure what they have thus far. Only real men have the inner strength to take on a hostile world and say to its face, "Laugh then—only men can endure it. Slander then—only a coward is shaken by it." They will stand up in the crowd, be spat at, scorned, mocked, and dismissed as fools.

In the meantime, a corps of disciplined fighters has rallied behind the Party's banner. They know not only how to use their mind but also their fists when someone threatens their lives or the movement. Let them be put under bloody terror, let them be hunted down by the police and the courts, let them be sent gangs of red murderers— do we imagine that men who have braved scorn and slander, who have faced down lies and ridicule, are now going to weaken under violence?

Quite the opposite! When it comes to defending a new ideal, the use of these methods by an adversary is a sure sign that those men are on the right track. If these methods were not used against them, they might now and then suspect themselves of having gone astray. But terror tactics provide them with the proof that the enemy has recognized them and that he hates them, simply because he fears them. Blood only further cements the unity of the movement. The leader and the men now form an indivisible body, a revolutionary phalanx, against which nothing can be seriously done anymore.

So it has been with all revolutionary uprisings of the past, and so it is with the revolutionary movement we serve. It is there. It can no longer be ignored. It has its own strength and its own ideal; it has its own united and disciplined followers. It will continue on its way un- deterred, because it is aware of the goal to be achieved and never loses sight of it, whatever detours it may want or need to take to get there. And in the end the enemy will realize that his methods have failed.

Meanwhile, people's convictions have also changed. The move- ment, in its years of relentless struggle, was not without leaving its mark on the people's soul. It has continued to act, mobilizing the masses, stirring them up, setting the people in motion. Today's Ger- man people can no longer be compared to those of 1918. The au- thority of the ruling system has declined. And as it has declined, the strength of the opposition has risen. What does it mean to take us National Socialists to court? It would make sense if the people looked up to these courts with the same childlike trust that the Miller of Sanssouci had for the judges of Berlin.[149] Even if the common man

---

[149] The Miller of Sanssouci is a legendary figure in German folklore. In the legend, King Frederick II wanted to buy the miller's workshop as it was an eyesore in the view of the king's summer residence. The miller refused, and the king threatened him with seizing the property without any compensation unless he agreed to sell the mill. The miller replied with a line to the effect of, "Of course you could . . . if it were not for the judges in Berlin." This blind trust in the impartial justice of the courts made the king have a change of heart, and so he allowed the miller to keep his property.

could still tell himself that the courts are the sanctuary of justice and that the men on the opposition were sentenced to severe punishments by these courts, then these penalties would, for the popular conscience, have something shameful and defamatory in them.

But when a court all but acquits a Barmat, [150] so to speak, and then sentences a National Socialist to a long prison term, the people cannot accept it. In the end, the common man says to himself, "Oh, I see how it is. Either we put the crooks away, or we put the honest men behind bars, because just as the criminal is a threat to the decent man, the decent man is a threat to the criminal."

The system's authority has diminished. Of course, the system does not want to acknowledge this, but it has to come to terms with it a little more with each passing day. The time is coming when the center of gravity will shift to the opposition, and the government will find itself isolated from the people. The struggle will thus be settled in the minds of the people, and it will also be settled very quickly in terms of power politics.

Slander is of no help any longer; in slandering the movement, one slanders the best elements of the people. Let its leaders be reviled, and the people will rise up in their millions and declare, "These men are ours. And whoever insults them insults us. Their honor is our honor."

People react when a National Socialist is put behind bars; when one is arrested in his home at night, they feel the same way as the common man who can no longer pay his taxes.

The final phase has begun. The movement can no longer be silenced, nor can it be brought down by lies, nor can it be cut down with violence. Wherever it is struck, the people shout, "I have been struck," and where a man of the movement is slandered, millions cry out, "That's us!" When one of the activists is gunned down in a dark street, the masses rise up and declare menacingly, "A hundred thousand men today wear the dead man's face and sit in judgment."

---

[150] This refers to the Barmat scandal of 1925 in the Weimar Republic. The Barmats were five brothers—from a Jewish family—who reaped millions and millions of Reichsmark through corruption, war profiteering, fraud, bribery, and other financial misdeeds. This is one of many scandals in the history of Weimar Germany involving Jews who abused and defrauded government systems, and by extension the German taxpayer, to make illegal profits for themselves. Ultimately, while all five brothers were arrested, only two were convicted, and each was sentenced to less than a year in incarceration, despite their guilt.

There is only one way out: the unconditional surrender of the enemy to the intellectual strength of the opposition, because he sees no other recourse but to submit to its principles—not in order to serve this ideal, but on the contrary, to corrupt it. Everyone has his own ideal. When someone has served pacifism all his life, he cannot suddenly be filled with a warmongering conviction. Someone who has fought for democracy for twenty years does not turn into a reactionary overnight. Someone who has spent decades trying to undermine the state cannot suddenly become its supporter. He can pretend, and he can put on a false mask.

All of a sudden, the Social Democrat, who for twelve years had taken care to keep the German people anesthetized, stands up gesticulating like a madman before the masses and shouts, "Germany is waking up!" Suddenly, these old special interest groups remember the people again. Then they call themselves the people's party. This is our German drama: We have three people's parties but no people.[151] They all prefix their names with the word "people." When their old name is abused and compromised, they abolish it altogether and take on a new one. For decades they fought under the banner of democracy—and as soon as democracy no longer holds sway, they suddenly call themselves state parties.[152]

They remain the same; they would just like to continue their old politics using new slogans. Behind them are the same putrefied minds, containing the same outdated ideas. But this no longer has any effect on the people. The old names are compromised, and when they give themselves a new name, the people compare them to that sort of people who like to change their surnames when it becomes embarrassing. This is exactly what conmen and Jews do. If someone is listed as "Meier" in criminal records, then he changes his name to "Müller." Or if someone comes from Galicia with the name "Mandelbaum," then once in Germany he changes it to "Elbau."[153]

---

[151] In the Weimar Republic, there were roughly forty different political parties with various names and various ideologies. Goebbels, perhaps speaking loosely, says there were three people's parties; however, we know today there were at least six major "people's parties." Nonetheless, the sentiment of his statement remains true.

[152] One such "state party" was the German State Party, which was politically centrist and supported the Weimar Republic.

[153] Galicia here denotes a region of east Central Europe, north of the Carpathian Mountains (not the region of Spain sharing the same name). Moreover, the personal names that are being changed (Meier and Mandelbaum) are strongly associated with

For twelve years, they have trampled on the nation, trampled on the honor of the people, spat on the fatherland, mocked and besmirched it; now they suddenly remember the stoically suffering people again, and now, in one fell swoop, they are uncompromising patriots on the attack against treason and pacifism. Now they want to get the battleships and the nation on a war footing, as they declare with utter conviction, "We cannot go on like this! We have to give the nation its due." Like pirates carrying contraband, they sail under a false flag. They have not even the slightest intention of saving the people; they only want to make the people's uprising serve the carcass that is their own party.

But they will soon recognize that this too is futile. And then they lose their composure and give up their peace of mind. Once these people, especially Jews, have lost their composure and peace of mind, they begin to behave foolishly. One notices how poorly they are doing, and despite their appearance of dignity, one can see their bitter tears flowing. They would like to play Goliath in front of the public. They pretend things are going well for them. They tell each other things like, "Do not get scared. Do not get nervous. No panicking about Hitler. Everything is not so bad." They scream, "We are not afraid!" However, it is the same for them as it is for the young boy who has to spend the night in a dark forest and shouts aloud, "I am not afraid," in an attempt to exorcise his own fear.

The National Socialist movement also had to go through the various phases of this development, both as a whole and in its individual units. Everywhere, attempts have been made to silence it, to burden it with threats, and to break it by force. And today, the only way to put an end to National Socialism in Germany is to take up its themes and demands and campaign against it.

In the fall of 1927, the National Socialist movement in Berlin was between the second and third phases of this development. The press was still trying to silence it with lies, but it was obviously not working. Then they resorted to violence, but after three months of fighting, the movement had broken through this menacing threat, too. The Party's victorious march was now unstoppable. National Socialism had taken hold. It could set about consolidating its positions, and

---

Jews; thus, the implication is Jews change their names to "assimilate" and deceive the host population.

having broken through the narrow boundaries of party politics, set out on a new course of conquest.

*   *   *

Der Angriff had now become the popular vehicle for our political views. Without worry or hindrance, we could spread our opinions in it. The language was striking and unmistakable, and the people listened. This was how the common man on the street liked to speak in the workplace, on the bus, and in the subway; the demands we raised were marked by the people's cries of indignation, and the people took up this cry.

"*Our* newspaper": that was what the Party members and supporters called *Der Angriff.* Everyone felt like a co-owner of this paper. Everyone was convinced that it could not have existed without his assistance. If the newspaper ever made a profit, it was expected to be used entirely for the benefit of the movement. In Berlin, *Der Angriff* was the only newspaper that was not submissively dependent on capitalism. None of us profited from it, only the movement itself.

It has remained that way to this day. We have worked hard to prevent the paper from becoming a private capitalist enterprise. Each contributor is paid according to his ability and in proportion to his work. But the paper itself belongs to the Party and therefore to every single member of the Party. Those who work for the paper serve the Party, not only in terms of political activity but also financially. Any improvement, any increase in the number of subscribers or in sales per issue on the street immediately contributes to a leap forward. As a result, the paper became more and more important, and although there was no chance of making a profit at the time, within three months we had managed to cover our operating costs. We only had to worry about how we could liquidate the heavy burden of debt we had taken on to found it, partly as a party and partly as private individuals.

Sometimes we had to get involved in risky financial operations. We, who did not understand much about finance, became sophisticated users of credit and borrowing. We unplugged one hole to plug another. We used every trick in the book to balance our financial statements, and now we had to be careful not to let the outside world know about the paper's sometimes dramatic financial situation.

We rely on nobody!

We can admit today that we were often at the end of our rope, but we always found a way out of every situation, even if by desperate means. We kept our spirits up and carried on in the hope that, in the long run, fate would be more kind to us.

One should not believe that the worries caused by these little daily miseries have turned us into pessimistic misanthropes. On the contrary, we were all far too young to lose heart for even a single moment, and had gradually become so accustomed to the tragedy of our situation that we saw it as a normal, one might almost say ideal, state of affairs. With a healthy sense of humor, we extricated ourselves from every critical situation. We laughed more than we brooded.

If we look back today at the entire development of the National Socialist movement, from the small, insignificant sect to the large, imposing party for the masses, we will always come back to the same conclusion: it is beautiful, and a source of satisfaction, to find oneself on the verge of fulfilling one's goals. But it is even more beautiful and even more satisfying to begin the fight for great goals, and despite the desperation of an unbearable situation, to find the strength and the faith to set to work, no matter how senseless, absurd, and pointless it may seem.

We were anything but dark, savage putschists. That was how the press liked to portray us. Most National Socialist leaders are young German men who came to politics as a result of the hardships of the times. It is the German youth who, having recognized that old age had become incapable of overcoming the grave miseries of our time, took up politics and gave it that character of dignity, which today distinguishes it from that of all other countries.

With unashamed insouciance, we took up public affairs. We began our work with a youthful temperament; it is only thanks to this youthful spirit that it has not remained unfruitful.

The youth rose up against an aging political situation that had become unbearable for them. They thawed the political waters and broke open the dams that kept German post-war politics from flowing freely. The youth have awakened spirits, warmed hearts, and shaken consciences. If there is still hope for a different future in Germany today, to whom do we owe it if not to ourselves and our movement?

*　　　*　　　*

There are days in a man's life when one would like to believe that all fortune or all misfortune had made an appointment to meet at the same time. One could thus come to the conclusion that, through a surplus of fortune, he is now requited for previous misfortune, or through a surplus of misfortune, now afflicted for previous good fortune. Fate has saved all its pleasant or unpleasant surprises for this moment and is now pouring them out in abundance.

For the movement in Berlin and for me personally, that day was October 29th, 1927. It was my thirtieth birthday. From the early hours of the morning, pleasant surprises poured in. The second letter I received at midday was from the police headquarters informing me that the ban on speaking in public, imposed on me more than four months earlier, had been lifted, with the stipulation that I could speak at public meetings provided that the police department, when notified in advance, had granted permission. It was an unexpected stroke of luck. The massive turnout at the meetings was now going to become an inexorable storm of rallies. In addition, the Party had obtained a new funding opportunity, and we could overcome our burdensome financial worries.

From that first birthday greeting on October 29th, 1927, the chain of happy events went on and on. Flowers, greetings, and telegrams poured in, spontaneously expressing the solidarity that had gradually been forged between Berlin's National Socialist movement and its leadership over the course of almost a year's struggle.

I spent the evening of that memorable day at the home of an old activist. I was invited, with an aura of mystery, to go for a walk that ended up, without it seeming suspicious to me, in some establishment in the suburbs of Berlin.

Without suspecting anything, I entered the room with my companion, and one can imagine my surprise when I found all the Party members from Berlin behind the closed doors. They had improvised a birthday party in my honor, and the Party members did not fail to bring their own surprises.

Berlin's popular humor was expressed in a striking way. I was ceremoniously handed an officially patented Isidor mask: "Perfectly faithful to the constitution and protects you from bludgeoning!"[154] There was a flurry of congratulatory messages from the SA and its political departments, written in a pure Berlin dialect, with the natural wit peculiar to the capital.

A Party official handed me a huge parcel; I was stunned to see that it contained the files of two and a half thousand new *Der Angriff* subscribers as a birthday present, which the entire Party had collected in two months, unbeknownst to me, in the course of tireless promotional work.

But that was not all. These poor penniless people had organized a collection among themselves and gave me a birthday present of almost two thousand marks. This enabled me to settle the most pressing debts. The backlog was cleared for new political work.

Finally, an SA man approached me and handed me a sealed envelope. It contained torn up promissory notes to the value of two thousand marks, which I had taken upon myself to help found *Der Angriff*.

---

[154] "Isidor" was the nickname Goebbels had given to Bernhard Weiss, the Jewish deputy chief of the Berlin police during the Weimar Republic. He would frequently sue Goebbels and try to prevent him from speaking in public.

Approved by the police department!

A briefly worded note informed me that these debts had been canceled.

Suddenly, all our financial worries were over. *Der Angriff* was no longer in debt, and the movement now had a rainy day fund. Our newspaper had grown its subscriber base, and in fact its future was guaranteed. My ban on public speaking had been lifted by the police department. In short, all the prerequisites were in place to resume work with new vigor and to lead the Party during the coming winter, toward new successes and new victories.

As unexpected as it was, all the worries and hardships we had endured for the movement were rewarded. Our auspicious star in the sky reappeared. The crises we had long since overcome on the inside were also resolved on the outside. Solid rapport was re-established within the Party, and the organization consolidated; we could undertake new political actions, without being hindered in our freedom of movement by any financial concern. The political leadership started taking initiative again, and their time and energy were no longer monopolized by petty financial worries. I myself became a free man again and could once more publicly devote myself to my political tasks.

That evening, an SA squad gave an amateur performance which, in its touching simplicity and artistic matter-of-factness, moved the audience to tears. The evolution of a German worker from communism to National Socialism was depicted vividly on stage. The play was composed by an unknown SA man and performed by anonymous amateurs.

> National theater must spring from the nation itself, from the people, by the people, and by means of amateur theater. National theater must be the home of those dramatic works that are the bearers of a heroic conviction, of a great ideal, dramatic works that illustrate the National Socialist worldview. National theater must rise from the people and belong to them, not to the unwashed masses.

One of the amateur performers began the play with that preface. The performance ended with a unanimous, stunning expression of trust. In the end, the room was plunged into darkness. An SA man stepped to the front of the stage with the Party flag draped around him and declaimed a poem dedicated to us all, vowing in captivating, fiery verse that we would never tire of fighting, and that we were determined to follow the struggle to victory with new means and new methods.

> We Berliners need a guy who beats the drum with verve, not so much for us as for the morons on the outside who don't want to get it. . . . Because we know you're the guy for us, and when one of those brothers comes to yell at you and spit at you, don't worry, we've got you covered. . . . So, honored Doctor, dear comrade, as we already said, we wish you all the best and all the happiness in the struggle, which will never be too crazy for our liking, especially with you here. . . . [155]

Thus was written the congratulatory letter for the occasion by an unknown SA man, full of crude humor and clever wit. With it, the supporters expressed their thanks for a year of work, worry, and struggle. We had overcome many difficulties. But we could now have the satisfying feeling that the struggle and worry had not been in vain.

*　　　*　　　*

---

[155] In the original text, Goebbels imitated the local Berlin dialect.

Authorized by the police department!

On Tuesday, November 8th, 1927, at eight o'clock in the evening, at the Orpheum Neukölln, 32–38 Hasenheide Street. Dr. Goebbels will speak on the topic:
"The German People's Dance of Death."
Come one, come all!

Over the following week, this poster adorned every bulletin board in the Reich's capital. The public was astonished to learn that the oppressed and gagged National Socialist movement had been resurrected.

Banned but not dead! This slogan found glorious confirmation on that decisive Tuesday evening, when, at 7 P.M., in front of the Orpheum on Hasenheide Street, in the middle of a proletarian district, on the eve of the anniversary of the 1918 industrial revolt and the same day as Adolf Hitler's 1923 proclamation of national revolution in Munich, the crowd gathered, and shortly after the ticket offices opened, the Orpheum's large hall was teeming, and the police had to prevent more people from entering.

They had all hurried over, the early fighters of the National Socialist movement in Berlin—SA and SS men, permanent staff, supporters from near and far. The Party's Old Guard gathered to celebrate the reappearance of the National Socialist movement. Admittedly, the ban imposed by the police department had not yet been lifted; we had to wait almost six months for that wrong to be righted, but it had become ineffective. Harassment and coercive measures had proven powerless. The movement's relentless persistence had broken the shackles with which they had tried to bind it.

Coming from the workshop or the office, from the bright houses of the West or the dark courtyards of the unemployment offices, there they sat, the men of the Old Guard. With ardent hearts, they made a solemn vow to continue to devote themselves to the cause that we served unselfishly, with all our strength, and that no power in the world could force us to abandon.

Over terror and repression, over great difficulties and imprisonment, justice and truth triumphed, the flag of our faith once again blazing high. We can be bent but not broken. They may bring us to our knees, but we will never surrender!

We young National Socialists know what we are talking about. We are convinced that if we despair, Germany will be thrown into chaos. That is why we stand firm in defending our cause, however hopeless it may seem, and in doing so we truly live up to the demand that Richard Wagner once attached to being German: to do something for its own sake.[156]

Berlin is slowly waking up!

On October 29th, 1927, it became clear to even the naysayer and the skeptic that a new phase in the development of the National Socialist movement in Berlin had begun. That SA man, who stood strong and defiantly, draped in the National Socialist flag before a captivated audience, who gave free rein to his anger and indignation in a poem with words full of vigor, had expressed what was overflowing in the ardent heart of the Party's Old Guard:

Held together, 'round the banner brave and true, a bulwark of Teutonic might.
Heads held high, resolute, too! Trumpeter! Sound the call to fight!
Listen to the signals, Germans of the Reich! The Party in Berlin, they've banned!

---

[156] This is a paraphrased statement of Wagner that he expressed in his work *Deutsche Kunst und deutsche Politik* (1868).

They seek the battle, and we shall prevail; crushing red terror, firm we stand.

We shake the foundations of oppressive might, 'til the Jewish thrones are quaking,

And then, in our own way and right, we'll thank you for the making.[157]

---

[157] A more literal translation of the original German poem reads, "Held together, a rampart of Teutonic warriors gathered around the banner! / Keep your heads up, and keep your defiance! Trumpeter, sound the reveille! / Heed the signal, Germans of the Reich! The Party has been banned in Berlin! / They want a fight, so we will give it to them. We will break the red terror. / We will rock the very foundations of power until the Jewish thrones totter. / Then we will thank you in our own way!"

ENJOYED THIS BOOK?

TO READ MORE, VISIT US AT

ANTELOPEHILLPUBLISHING.COM